Magento 2 Development Quick Start Guide

Build better stores by extending Magento

Branko Ajzele

BIRMINGHAM - MUMBAI

Magento 2 Development Quick Start Guide

Commissioning Editor: Amarabha Banerjee
Acquisition Editor: Reshma Raman
Content Development Editor: Kirk Dsouza
Technical Editor: Vaibhav Dwivedi
Copy Editor: Safis Editing
Project Coordinator: Hardik Bhinde
Proofreader: Safis Editing
Indexer: Aishwarya Gangawane
Graphics: Alishon Mendonsa
Production Coordinator: Deepika Naik

First published: September 2018

Production reference: 1180918

Published by Packt Publishing Ltd.
Livery Place
35 Livery Street
Birmingham
B3 2PB, UK.

ISBN 978-1-78934-344-1

www.packtpub.com

`mapt.io`

Mapt is an online digital library that gives you full access to over 5,000 books and videos, as well as industry leading tools to help you plan your personal development and advance your career. For more information, please visit our website.

Why subscribe?

- Spend less time learning and more time coding with practical eBooks and Videos from over 4,000 industry professionals

- Improve your learning with Skill Plans built especially for you

- Get a free eBook or video every month

- Mapt is fully searchable

- Copy and paste, print, and bookmark content

Packt.com

Did you know that Packt offers eBook versions of every book published, with PDF and ePub files available? You can upgrade to the eBook version at `www.packt.com` and as a print book customer, you are entitled to a discount on the eBook copy. Get in touch with us at `customercare@packtpub.com` for more details.

At `www.packt.com`, you can also read a collection of free technical articles, sign up for a range of free newsletters, and receive exclusive discounts and offers on Packt books and eBooks.

Contributors

About the author

Branko Ajzele is a respected and highly accomplished software developer, book author, solution specialist, consultant, and team leader. He currently works for Interactive Web Solutions Ltd (iWeb), where he holds the role of senior developer and is the director of iWeb's Croatia office.

Branko holds several respected IT certifications, including Zend Certified PHP Engineer, Magento Certified Developer, Magento Certified Developer Plus, Magento Certified Solution Specialist, Magento 2 Certified Solution Specialist, Magento 2 Certified Professional Developer, to mention just a few.

He was crowned the e-commerce Developer of the Year by the Digital Entrepreneur Awards in October 2014 for his excellent knowledge and expertise in e-commerce development.

> *Special thanks to my supportive wife, Ivana, for her understanding when I took quite a bit of our family time for this endeavor.*

About the reviewer

Andrew "Pembo" Pemberton is a Certified Magento Developer with over 20 years' experience building websites. He is based in Stoke-on-Trent, UK and started building websites from the young age of 13. He has a degree in computer science from Staffordshire University.

Andrew is now the development director at iWeb (based in Stafford, UK), which, for over 20 years, has created industry-leading websites and now specializes in large scale Magento solutions and PIM-based projects for a wide range of clients.

Outside of his digital life, Andrew enjoys spending time with his family of pets, traveling with his wife, and being an avid gamer.

Packt is searching for authors like you

If you're interested in becoming an author for Packt, please visit authors.packtpub.com and apply today. We have worked with thousands of developers and tech professionals, just like you, to help them share their insight with the global tech community. You can make a general application, apply for a specific hot topic that we are recruiting an author for, or submit your own idea.

Table of Contents

Preface

Magento is a popular open source e-commerce platform written in PHP. It is used primarily for building web shops, though it can easily be used for other types of websites as well. With the help of its powerful web API, we can build robust solutions that satisfy modern-day application requirements.

By the end of this book, the reader should be familiar with configuration files, models, collections, blocks, controllers, events, observers, plugins, UI components and other building elements of Magento.

Who this book is for

This book is intended for PHP developers getting started with Magento v2.x development. Though compact in terms of page numbers, the book covers a wide range of functionality, allowing the reader to master day-to-day Magento skills in a clear and concise way. No previous Magento knowledge is required.

What this book covers

Chapter 1, *Understanding the Magento Architecture,* takes a look at some of the key Magento components. We will go through plugins and event observers and learn how they provide a powerful way of extending Magento, either by changing the behavior of existing functions or by running some follow-up code in response to certain events.

Chapter 2, *Working with Entities,* demonstrates how to differentiate between the three types of Magento models: non-persistable, persistable simple, and persistable EAV. We will take a look at the six different setup scripts and how they allow us a great deal of flexibility for schema and data management.

Chapter 3, *Understanding Web API,* shows the reader how to differentiate between types of web API users, authentication, and methods it provides. We will also take a look at how easy it is to create our own APIs with just a few lines of XML. We will see how the route definition allows for easy binding between what arrives via HTTP requests and what is executed in code, respecting the access list permissions in the process.

Chapter 4, *Building and Distributing Extensions*, discusses how to create a simple shipping module. We shall take a look at how easy it is to add specific shipping calculations as part of offline shipping methods. We will then package this module and distribute it via Packagist. This makes it easy for the end consumer to use our module with just a few simple console commands.

Chapter 5, *Developing for Admin*, walks the reader through building two very different screens in the Magento admin area. One utilizes the listing component, whereas the other utilizes the form component.

Chapter 6, *Developing for Storefront*, covers the bits and pieces involved in storefront development, which JS components make the most challenging part of. We will understand how to write new components, as well as how to override or bypass existing ones – an essential skill for any Magento developer, be it backend or frontend.

Chapter 7, *Customizing Catalog Behavior*, demonstrates building three distinctive functionalities, all of which relate to the catalog part of Magento. They demonstrate how easily Magento can be extended with new features without really overriding any of the core files. Using plugins and JS components are just some of the approaches we might take.

Chapter 8, *Customizing Checkout Experience*, demonstrates writing a small but functional order notes module. This will allow us to familiarize ourselves with an important aspect of customizing the checkout experience, the gist of which lies in understanding the checkout_index_index layout handle, the JavaScript window.checkoutConfig object, and uiComponent.

Chapter 9, *Customizing Customer Interactions*, walks the reader through building a small module that allows us to get a greater insight into Magento's customer data and sections mechanism. We will learn how to manage and build a single component, which will get used both on the customer's **My Account** page, as well as at the checkout.

To get the most out of this book

To get the most out of the book, the reader is expected to have:

- A degree of PHP **object-oriented programming** (**OOP**) knowledge
- A basic understanding of JavaScript and XML

Download the example code files

You can download the example code files for this book from your account at www.packtpub.com. If you purchased this book elsewhere, you can visit www.packtpub.com/support and register to have the files emailed directly to you.

You can download the code files by following these steps:

1. Log in or register at www.packtpub.com.
2. Select the **SUPPORT** tab.
3. Click on **Code Downloads & Errata**.
4. Enter the name of the book in the **Search** box and follow the onscreen instructions.

Once the file is downloaded, please make sure that you unzip or extract the folder using the latest version of:

- WinRAR/7-Zip for Windows
- Zipeg/iZip/UnRarX for Mac
- 7-Zip/PeaZip for Linux

The code bundle for the book is also hosted on GitHub at https://github.com/PacktPublishing/Magento-2-Quick-Start-Guide. In case there's an update to the code, it will be updated on the existing GitHub repository.

We also have other code bundles from our rich catalog of books and videos available at https://github.com/PacktPublishing. Check them out!

Code in Action

Visit the following link to check out videos of the code being run:

http://bit.ly/2D98D8q

Conventions used

There are a number of text conventions used throughout this book.

`CodeInText`: Indicates code words in text, database table names, folder names, filenames, file extensions, pathnames, dummy URLs, user input, and Twitter handles. Here is an example: "The default area is the frontend, as defined by the default argument under `modulestore/etc/di.xml`."

A block of code is set as follows:

```
const AREA_GLOBAL = 'global';
const AREA_FRONTEND = 'frontend';
const AREA_ADMINHTML = 'adminhtml';
const AREA_DOC = 'doc';
const AREA_CRONTAB = 'crontab';
const AREA_WEBAPI_REST = 'webapi_rest';
const AREA_WEBAPI_SOAP = 'webapi_soap';
```

When we wish to draw your attention to a particular part of a code block, the relevant lines or items are set in bold:

```
const AREA_GLOBAL = 'global';
const AREA_FRONTEND = 'frontend';
const AREA_ADMINHTML = 'adminhtml';
const AREA_DOC = 'doc';
const AREA_CRONTAB = 'crontab';
const AREA_WEBAPI_REST = 'webapi_rest';
const AREA_WEBAPI_SOAP = 'webapi_soap';
```

Any command-line input or output is written as follows:

```
 php bin/magento setup:install \
--db-host="/Applications/MAMP/tmp/mysql/mysql.sock" \
--db-name=magelicious \
```

Bold: Indicates a new term, an important word, or words that you see onscreen. For example, words in menus or dialog boxes appear in the text like this. Here is an example: "The **tab** element of the file, which is used to provide a sidebar menu presence under **Magento admin Stores | Settings | Configuration**, is a nice example."

 Warnings or important notes appear like this.

 Tips and tricks appear like this.

Get in touch

Feedback from our readers is always welcome.

General feedback: Email feedback@packtpub.com and mention the book title in the subject of your message. If you have questions about any aspect of this book, please email us at questions@packtpub.com.

Errata: Although we have taken every care to ensure the accuracy of our content, mistakes do happen. If you have found a mistake in this book, we would be grateful if you would report this to us. Please visit www.packtpub.com/submit-errata, selecting your book, clicking on the Errata Submission Form link, and entering the details.

Piracy: If you come across any illegal copies of our works in any form on the Internet, we would be grateful if you would provide us with the location address or website name. Please contact us at copyright@packtpub.com with a link to the material.

If you are interested in becoming an author: If there is a topic that you have expertise in and you are interested in either writing or contributing to a book, please visit authors.packtpub.com.

Reviews

Please leave a review. Once you have read and used this book, why not leave a review on the site that you purchased it from? Potential readers can then see and use your unbiased opinion to make purchase decisions, we at Packt can understand what you think about our products, and our authors can see your feedback on their book. Thank you!

For more information about Packt, please visit packtpub.com.

Understanding the Magento Architecture

Building web shops is a challenging and tedious job, and even more so if a platform you are working on is limited via features, extensibility, and the overall ecosystem it provides. Choosing the right platform can often make the difference between a project's success or failure. The abundance of available e-commerce software, from SaaS to self-hosted solutions, does not really make it an easy choice.

The Magento e-commerce platform has been around for over 10 years now. With its first stable release dating back to March 2008, it immediately caught the attention of developers as an extensible and feature-rich open source platform. Over time, Magento established itself as not just a stunning technical and feature-rich platform, but as a robust ecosystem as well. By allowing developers to validate their real-world skills through the Magento certification program, certain standards have been put into effect, making it easier for merchants to better recognize their solution partners. Training courses have been further provided for other roles in e-commerce business as well, such as merchants, marketers, system administrators, and business analysts.

In this chapter, we will take a look at some of the key *must-knows* about Magento:

- Installing Magento
- Modes
- Areas
- Request flow processing
- Modules
- Cache
- Dependency injection
- Plugins

- Events and observers
- Console commands
- Cron jobs

To keep things compact as we move forward, let's assume the following throughout this book:

- We are working on the `magelicious.loc` project
- We are referring to our project root directory as `<PROJECT_DIR>`
- We are referring to the `<PROJECT_DIR>/app/code/Magelicious` directory as `<MAGELICIOUS_DIR>`
- We are referring to Magento's `vendor/magento` directory as `<MAGENTO_DIR>`
- We have a running LAMP/MAMP/WAMP stack (Apache, MySQL, PHP) that is compliant with Magento's requirements
- We have a Composer package manager installed
- We have access to crontab (Linux, MacOS) or Task Scheduler (Windows)

 AMPPS is an easy to use, all in one LAMP/MAMP/WAMP software stack from Softaculous, which enables Apache, MySQL, and PHP. With AMPPS, you can even install Magento 2.x by the click of a button, which means it comes loaded with all the right PHP extensions. While it isn't suited for production purposes, it comes in handy for quickly kicking the development environment. See `http://www.ampps.com/` for more information. Consult the devdocs (`https://devdocs.magento.com`) for Magento technology stack requirements.

Technical requirements

You will need to have basic knowledge of PHP, OOP, JavaScript, and XML. You will also need Apache, MySQL, and AMPPS installed on your system to execute the codes.

The code files of this chapter can be found on GitHub:
`https://github.com/PacktPublishing/Magento-2-Quick-Start-Guide`.

Check out the following video to see the Code in Action:

`http://bit.ly/2D8kOlF`.

Installing Magento

The Magento platform comes in two flavors:

- **Magento Open Source**: The free version, targeting small businesses
- **Magento Commerce**: The commercial version, targeting small, medium, or enterprise businesses

The difference between the two comes mainly in the form of extra modules that were added to the *Commerce* version, whereas all the coding concepts and core features remain the same. It goes to say that any knowledge we obtain through following Magento Open Source examples is fully applicable to anyone working on Magento Commerce.

There are several ways that we can obtain *source files* for Magento Open Source:

- Source file archive (`.zip`, `.tar.gz`, `.tar.bz2`), available at `https://magento.com`
- Git repository, available at `https://github.com/magento/magento2`
- Composer repository, available at `https://repo.magento.com`

Obtaining source files via a CLI from the composer repository is our preferred method. Assuming we are within the empty `<PROJECT_DIR>` directory, we can kick off this process via the following command:

```
composer create-project --repository-url=https://repo.magento.com/
magento/project-community-edition .
```

The dot (`.`) at the end of this command this tells the composer to pull the files into a current directory.

Once the Composer process is finished, we can start installing Magento. There are two ways we can install Magento:

- **Via the Web Setup Wizard**: The graphical, browser-based process
- **Via the command line**: The command-line-based process

Knowing how to install Magento via the command line is an essential skill in day-to-day development, as the majority of development requires the developer to tackle various `bin/magento` commands—not to mention the command line approach is somewhat faster and easily scripted.

Let's install Magento with the built-in `php bin/magento setup:install` command and a few of the required installation options as follows:

```
php bin/magento setup:install \
--db-host="/Applications/MAMP/tmp/mysql/mysql.sock" \
--db-name=magelicious \
--db-user=root \
--db-password=root \
--admin-firstname=John \
--admin-lastname=Doe \
--admin-email=john@magelicious.loc \
--admin-user=john \
--admin-password=jrdJ%0i9a69n
```

After the preceding command has been executed, we should begin to see console progress, starting with something like the following:

```
Starting Magento installation:
File permissions check...
[Progress: 1 / 513]
Required extensions check...
[Progress: 2 / 513]
Enabling Maintenance Mode...
[Progress: 3 / 513]
Installing deployment configuration...
[Progress: 4 / 513]
Installing database schema:
Schema creation/updates:
Module 'Magento_Store':
[Progress: 5 / 513]
```

While it might take up to a few minutes, a successful installation should end with a message that's similar to the following:

```
[Progress: 508 / 513]
Installing admin user...
[Progress: 509 / 513]
Caches clearing:
Cache cleared successfully
[Progress: 510 / 513]
Disabling Maintenance Mode:
[Progress: 511 / 513]
Post installation file permissions check...
For security, remove write permissions from these directories:
'/Users/branko/Projects/magelicious/app/etc'
[Progress: 512 / 513]
Write installation date...
[Progress: 513 / 513]
```

```
[SUCCESS]: Magento installation complete.
[SUCCESS]: Magento Admin URI: /admin_mxq00c
Nothing to import.
```

Right after installation, our first step should be to set Magento to `developer` mode by using the following command:

php bin/magento deploy:mode:set developer

We will take a closer look at Magento *modes* soon; for now, this is to be taken as is.

 Magento automatically assigns an admin URL during console installation, unless explicitly specified through the `install` command via the `--backend-frontname` option.

 Out of all the installation options listed, only the following are actually required: `--admin-firstname`, `--admin-lastname`, `--admin-email`, `--admin-user`, and `--admin-password`. It is worth taking some time to read through the official Magento documentation (`https://devdocs.magento.com`) and looking at what the rest of the installation options have to offer.

If all went well during the Magento installation, we should be able to open the storefront and admin in our browser.

Modes

Modes play a crucial role in Magento's development and deployment processes. They are handled by the `deploy` module, which can be found under the `<MAGENTO_DIR>/module-deploy` directory.

The built-in `php bin/magento` command provides us with the following `deploy` commands:

```
deploy
  deploy:mode:set Set application mode.
   deploy:mode:show Displays current application mode.
```

We already used the `deploy:mode:set developer` command to switch from `default` to `developer` mode.

Magento differentiates between following three modes:

- `default`: The default *after-install* mode:
  - Not optimized for production
  - Symlinks to static view files are published to the `pub/static` directory
  - Errors and exceptions are not shown to the user, as they are logged to the filesystem
  - Should avoid using it
- `developer`: For development systems only:
  - Symlinks to static view files are published to the `pub/static` directory
  - Provides verbose logging
  - Enables automatic code compilation
  - Enables enhanced debugging
  - Slowest performance
- `production`: For production systems:
  - Errors and exceptions are not shown to the user, as they are logged to the filesystem
  - Static view files are not materialized, as they are served from the cache only
  - Automatic code file compilation is disabled, as new or updated files are not written to the filesystem
  - Enabling and disabling the cache types is not possible from the Magento admin
  - Fastest performance

 Carefully balancing **developer** mode with some of the cache types being **enabled/disabled** can provide optimal performance during development.

Areas

The area is a logical component that organizes code for optimized request processing. While the majority of the time we don't really have to code anything specific regarding areas, understanding them is key to understanding Magento.

The `Magento\Framework\App\Area` class `AREA_*` constants hint at the following areas:

```
const AREA_GLOBAL = 'global';
const AREA_FRONTEND = 'frontend';
const AREA_ADMINHTML = 'adminhtml';
const AREA_DOC = 'doc';
const AREA_CRONTAB = 'crontab';
const AREA_WEBAPI_REST = 'webapi_rest';
const AREA_WEBAPI_SOAP = 'webapi_soap';
```

By doing a lookup for the `<argument name="areas"` string across all of the `<MAGENTO_DIR>` `di.xml` files, we can see that five of these areas have been explicitly added to the `areas` argument of the `Magento\Framework\App\AreaList` class:

- `adminhtml` via `<MAGENTOI_DIR>/module-backend/etc/di.xml`
- `webapi_rest` via `<MAGENTOI_DIR>/module-webapi/etc/di.xml`
- `webapi_soap` via `<MAGENTOI_DIR>/magento/module-webapi/etc/di.xml`
- `frontend` via `<MAGENTOI_DIR>/magento/module-store/etc/di.xml`
- `crontab` via `<MAGENTOI_DIR>/magento/module-cron/etc/di.xml`

The default area is `frontend`, as defined by the `default` argument under `module-store/etc/di.xml`. The `global` area is used as a fallback for files that are absent in the `adminhtml` and `frontend` areas.

Let's take a closer look at the `<MAGENTO_DIR>/module-webapi/etc/di.xml` file:

```xml
<type name="Magento\Framework\App\AreaList">
    <arguments>
        <argument name="areas" xsi:type="array">
            <item name="webapi_rest" xsi:type="array">
                <item name="frontName" xsi:type="string">rest</item>
            </item>
            <item name="webapi_soap" xsi:type="array">
                <item name="frontName" xsi:type="string">soap</item>
            </item>
        </argument>
    </arguments>
</type>
```

The frontName is what sometimes appears at the front of the URL, whereas the area name is used internally to refer to the area in configuration files. Different areas defined by Magento can contain different code for processing URLs and requests. This allows Magento to load only the dependent code for the specified area.

When developing modules, we define which resources are visible and accessible in a given area. This way, we get to control the specific area behavior if needed. An example of one such behavior might be the definition of the **event** observer under the frontend area for customer_save_after event. This observer would only trigger on customer save operations that are triggered from the storefront, which usually indicates a customer register action. The adminhtml area operations, such as Magento admin manually creating a customer, would fail to trigger this observer, as it was defined under the frontend area.

On occasion, we might need to run some code that only executes under certain areas. In such cases, *emulation* helps us emulate any store programmatically. The Magento\Store\Model\App\Emulation class provides the startEnvironmentEmulation and stopEnvironmentEmulation methods, which we can use for this purpose, as per the following partial example:

```
protected $storeRepository;
protected $emulation;

public function __construct(
    \Magento\Store\Api\StoreRepositoryInterface $storeRepository,
    \Magento\Store\Model\App\Emulation $emulation
) {
    $this->storeRepository = $storeRepository;
    $this->emulation = $emulation;
}

public function test() {
    $store = $this->storeRepository->get('store-to-emulate');
    $this->emulation->startEnvironmentEmulation(
        $store->getId(),
        \Magento\Framework\App\Area::AREA_FRONTEND
    );
    // Code to execute in emulated environment
    $this->emulation->stopEnvironmentEmulation();
}
```

While it is not a common thing to do, we can further register new areas ourselves. This is easily done by using the module's di.xml.

Request flow processing

URLs in Magento have the format of
`<AreaFrontName>/<VendorName>/<ModuleName>/<ControllerName>/<ActionName>`
, but this does not mean that we actually use the area, vendor, or module name in the URL
any time we wish to access a certain controller. For example, the area for a request is
defined by the first request path segment, such as *admin* for `adminhtml` area, and *none* for
`frontend` area.

We use the *router* class to assign a URL to a corresponding *controller* and its *action*. The
router's `match` method finds a matching controller, which is determined by an incoming
request.

Conceptually, creating a new *router* is as simple as doing the following:

1. Inject the new `item` under the `routerList argument` of the
   `Magento\Framework\App\RouterList` type via the `di.xml` file.
2. Create a router file (by using the `match` method, which *implements*
   `\Magento\Framework\App\RouterInterface`).
3. Return an instance of `\Magento\Framework\App\ActionInterface`.

By doing a lookup for the `name="routerList"` string across all of the `<MAGENTO_DIR>`
`di.xml` files, we can see the following *router* definitions:

- `Magento\Robots\Controller\Router (robots)`
- `Magento\Cms\Controller\Router (cms)`
- `Magento\UrlRewrite\Controller\Router (urlrewrite)`
- `Magento\Framework\App\Router\Base (standard)`
- `Magento\Framework\App\Router\DefaultRouter (default)`
- `Magento\Backend\App\Router (admin)`

Let's take a closer look at the `robots` router under `<MAGENTO_DIR>/module-robots.`
`etc/frontend/di.xml` injects the new item under the `routerList` argument as follows:

```
<type name="Magento\Framework\App\RouterList">
    <arguments>
        <argument name="routerList" xsi:type="array">
            <item name="robots" xsi:type="array">
                <item name="class"
xsi:type="string">Magento\Robots\Controller\Router</item>
                <item name="disable" xsi:type="boolean">false</item>
                <item name="sortOrder" xsi:type="string">10</item>
```

```
                </item>
            </argument>
        </arguments>
    </type>
```

The `Magento\Robots\Controller\Router` class has been further defined as per the following partial extract:

```
class Router implements \Magento\Framework\App\RouterInterface {
    // Magento\Framework\App\ActionFactory
    private $actionFactory;
    // Magento\Framework\App\Router\ActionList
    private $actionList;
    // Magento\Framework\App\Route\ConfigInterface
    private $routeConfig;

    public function match(\Magento\Framework\App\RequestInterface $request)
    {
        $identifier = trim($request->getPathInfo(), '/');
        if ($identifier !== 'robots.txt') {
            return null;
        }

        $modules = $this->routeConfig->getModulesByFrontName('robots');
        if (empty($modules)) {
            return null;
        }

        $actionClassName = $this->actionList->get($modules[0], null,
'index', 'index');
        $actionInstance = $this->actionFactory->create($actionClassName);
        return $actionInstance;
    }
}
```

The `match` method checks if the `robots.txt` file was requested and returns the instance of the matched `\Magento\Framework\App\ActionInterface` type. By following this simple implementation, we can easily create the route of our own.

Conceptually, creating a new *controller* is as simple as doing the following:

1. Register a route via `router.xml`.
2. Create an *abstract* controller file (as an *abstract* class, which *extends* `\Magento\Framework\App\Action\Action`).

3. Create an *action* controller file (which *extends* the main controller file with the `execute` method, and *implements* `\Magento\Framework\App\ActionInterface`).

4. Return an instance of `\Magento\Framework\Controller\ResultInterface`.

> The separation of the controller into the *main* and *action* controller files is not a technical requirement, but rather a recommended organizational one. Magento does this across the majority of its modules.

By doing a lookup for the `<route` string across the `<MAGENTO_DIR>` `routes.xml` files, we can see that Magento uses hundreds of `route` definitions, which are spread across its modules. Each `route` represents one controller.

Let's take a closer look at one of Magento's controllers, `<MAGENTO_DIR>/module-customer`, which maps to the `http://magelicious.loc/customer/address/form` URL. The route itself is registered via `frontend/di.xml` under the `standard` router with a `customer` ID and a `customer frontName`, as follows:

```
<router id="standard">
    <route id="customer" frontName="customer">
        <module name="Magento_Customer" />
    </route>
</router>
```

The *abstract* controller file `Controller/Address.php` is defined partially as follows:

```
abstract class Address extends \Magento\Framework\App\Action\Action {
    // The rest of the code...
}
```

The *abstract* controller is where we want to add functionality and dependencies that are shared across all of the child *action* controllers.

We can further see three different *action* controllers defined within the subdirectory which has the same name as the *abstract* class. The `Controller/Address` directory contains six action controllers: `Delete.php`, `Edit.php`, `Form.php`, `FormPost.php`, `Index.php`, and `NewAction.php`. Let's take a closer look at the following partial `Form.php` file's content:

```
class Form extends \Magento\Customer\Controller\Address {
    public function execute() {
        /** @var \Magento\Framework\View\Result\Page $resultPage */
        $resultPage = $this->resultPageFactory->create();
        $navigationBlock =
$resultPage->getLayout()->getBlock('customer_account_navigation');
```

```
        if ($navigationBlock) {
            $navigationBlock->setActive('customer/address');
        }
        return $resultPage;
    }
}
```

The example here uses the `create` method of the injected `Magento\Framework\View\Result\PageFactory` type to create a new page result. The various types of *controller* results can be found within the `<MAGENTO_DIR>/framework` directory:

- `Magento\Framework\Controller\Result\Json`
- `Magento\Framework\Controller\Result\Raw`
- `Magento\Framework\Controller\Result\Redirect`
- `Magento\Framework\Controller\Result\Forward`
- `Magento\Framework\View\Result\Layout`
- `Magento\Framework\View\Result\Page`

We can take the unified way of creating result instances by using the `create` method of `\Magento\Framework\Controller\ResultFactory`. The `ResultFactory` defines the `TYPE_*` constant for each of the mentioned controller result types:

```
const TYPE_JSON = 'json';
const TYPE_RAW = 'raw';
const TYPE_REDIRECT = 'redirect';
const TYPE_FORWARD = 'forward';
const TYPE_LAYOUT = 'layout';
const TYPE_PAGE = 'page';
```

Keeping these constants in mind, we can easily write our action controller code as follows:

```
$resultRedirect =
$this->resultFactory->create(ResultFactory::TYPE_REDIRECT);
$resultRedirect->setPath('adminhtml/*/index');
return $resultRedirect;
```

 A quick lookup for the `$this->resultFactory->` create string, across the entire `<MAGENTO_DIR>` directory, can give us lots of examples of how to use the `ResultFactory` for our own code.

Modules

The *top-level* Magento structure is rather simple. When we strip away *(seemingly) non-relevant files* such as licenses, sample files, and changelogs, what remains looks much like the following:

```
app/
    code/
    design/
    etc/
        config.php
        env.php
bin/
composer.json
composer.lock
dev/
generated/
index.php
lib/
phpserver/
pub/
    static/
        adminhtml/
        frontend/
setup/
update/
var/
    cache/
    log/
    page_cache/
    view_preprocessed/
        pub/
            static/
                adminhtml/
                frontend/
vendor/
    composer/
    magento/
    symfony/
```

The app/code/<VendorName>/<ModuleName> directory, <MAGELICIOUS_DIR> for short, is where our custom code will reside.

When developer mode is enabled, we can manually clean the *cache*, *compilation*, and *static* files via the `rm -rf var/cache/* && rm -rf var/page_cache/* && rm -rf var/view_preprocessed/* && rm -rf generated/* && rm -rf pub/static/*` command. Under limited use cases, this can provide a faster development workflow.

The `vendor/magento` directory, `<MAGENTO_DIR>` for short, is where Magento source code resides, as per the following partial listing:

```
vendor/
    magento/
        composer/
        framework/
        language-de_de/
        language-en_us/
        magento-composer-installer/
        magento2-base/
        module-catalog/
        module-checkout/
        theme-adminhtml-backend/
        theme-frontend-blank/
        theme-frontend-luma/
```

The individual module directory is where things get interesting. Let's take a quick look at the structure of one of the simpler Magento modules, `<MAGENTO_DIR>/module-contact`:

```
Block/
Controller/
etc/
Helper/
i18n/
Model/
Test/
view/
composer.json
LICENSE.txt
LICENSE_AFL.txt
README.md
registration.php
```

This is by no means the final structure of the individual module. There are other directories the module can define, as we will see as we move forward throughout this book.

Creating the minimal module

Let's create the most minimal module there is in Magento. Our module will be called `Core` and it will belong to the `Magelicious` vendor. The formula for determining the directory of custom modules is `app/code/<VendorName>/<ModuleName>`, or in our case `<MAGELICIOUS_DIR>/Core`.

We start off by creating the `<MAGELICIOUS_DIR>/Core/registration.php` file with the following content:

```
\Magento\Framework\Component\ComponentRegistrar::register(
    \Magento\Framework\Component\ComponentRegistrar::MODULE,
    'Magelicious_Core',
    __DIR__
);
```

The `registration.php` file is essentially the entry point of our module. The `register` method of the `Magento\Framework\Component\ComponentRegistrar` class provides the ability to statically register components, whereas a component can be more than just a module, as defined via the following constants:

- `Magento\Framework\Component\ComponentRegistrar::MODULE`
- `Magento\Framework\Component\ComponentRegistrar::LIBRARY`
- `Magento\Framework\Component\ComponentRegistrar::THEME`
- `Magento\Framework\Component\ComponentRegistrar::LANGUAGE`

Next, we will create the `<MAGELICIOUS_DIR>/Core/etc/module.xml` file with the following content:

```
<config>
    <module name="Magelicious_Core" setup_version="1.0.0">
        <sequence>
            <module name="Magento_Store"/>
            <module name="Magento_Backend"/>
            <module name="Magento_Config"/>
        </sequence>
    </module>
</config>
```

The `name` and `setup_version` attributes of a `module` element are considered required. The sequence, on the other hand, is optional. We use it to define any potential dependencies around other Magento modules.

Finally, we add `composer.json` with the following content:

```json
{
    "name": "magelicious/module-core",
    "description": "The core module",
    "require": {
        "php": "^7.0.0"
    },
    "type": "magento2-module",
    "version": "1.0.0",
    "license": [
        "OSL-3.0",
        "AFL-3.0"
    ],
    "autoload": {
        "files": [
            "registration.php"
        ],
        "psr-4": {
            "Magelicious\\Core\\": ""
        }
    }
}
```

Magento supports the following `composer.json` types:

- `magento2-module` for modules
- `magento2-theme` for themes
- `magento2-language` for language packages
- `magento2-component` for general extensions that do not fit any of the other types

Though `composer.json` is not required for our custom module to be seen by Magento, it is recommended to add it to any component we are building.

You can trigger module installation by running the `php bin/magento module:enable Magelicious_Core` command, like so:

```
$ php bin/magento module:enable Magelicious_Core
The following modules have been enabled:
- Magelicious_Core

To make sure that the enabled modules are properly registered, run
'setup:upgrade'.
Cache cleared successfully.
Generated classes cleared successfully. Please run the 'setup:di:compile'
```

```
command to generate classes.
Info: Some modules might require static view files to be cleared. To do
this, run 'module:enable' with the --clear-static-content option to clear
them.
```

You can run the `php bin/magento setup:upgrade` command to trigger any install and/or update scripts that need to be triggered:

```
Cache cleared successfully
File system cleanup:
generated/code/Composer
generated/code/Magento
generated/code/Symfony
Updating modules:
Schema creation/updates:
Module 'Magento_Store':
...
Module 'Magento_CmsUrlRewrite':
Module 'Magelicious_Core':
Module 'Magento_ConfigurableImportExport':
...
Nothing to import.
```

This finishes our module installation.

 Creating the `<VendorName>/Core` module is often a good practice when working on a project with lots of custom `<VendorName>` modules. Used carefully, the `Core` module can provide common bits that are shared across several other modules. The **tab** element of the `system.xml` file, which is used to provide a *sidebar menu presence* under Magento's admin **Stores** | **Settings** | **Configuration**, is a nice example. Similarly, we can use it to provide top-level access resources for other modules to use.

To confirm our module was installed correctly, perform the following:

- Check the `<PROJECT_DIR>/app/etc/config.php` file for the `'Magelicious_Core' => 1` entry
- Check the `setup_module` table for the `Magelicious_Core 1.0.0 1.0.0` entry

At the moment, our module does absolutely nothing, aside from just sitting there. However, these few simple steps are the basis for us moving forward with Magento development, because the majority of things in Magento are done via a module, alongside other types of components, which we have already mentioned.

Cache

Magento makes extensive use of caching. The **System** | **Tools** | **Cache Management** section enables us to **Enable** | **Disable** | **Refresh** the cache from the comfort of the graphical interface. During development, the use of the console is more convenient and faster.

The following cache-related commands are supported:

```
cache
  cache:clean Cleans cache type(s)
  cache:disable Disables cache type(s)
  cache:enable Enables cache type(s)
  cache:flush Flushes cache storage used by cache type(s)
  cache:status Checks cache status
```

Out of the box, Magento Open Source comes with 14 different cache types. We can easily get the status of each cache type by running the `php bin/magento cache:status` command, which gives the following output:

```
Current status:
                     config: 0
                     layout: 0
                 block_html: 0
                collections: 0
                 reflection: 0
                     db_ddl: 0
                        eav: 0
      customer_notification: 0
           the_custom_cache: 1
         config_integration: 0
     config_integration_api: 0
                  full_page: 0
                  translate: 0
          config_webservice: 0
```

We can use the **enable** | **disable** | **clean** cache commands to impact one or more cache types at once.

 Disabled cache types are not cleaned. Use the `cache:flush` command with care, as flushing the cache type purges the entire cache storage. This, in turn, might affect other applications that are using the same storage.

If built-in cache types are not enough, we can always create our own.

Creating a new cache type in Magento is as easy as doing the following:

Create the `<MAGELICIOUS_DIR>/Core/etc/cache.xml` file with the following content:

```
<config>
    <type name="the_custom_cache" translate="label,description"
instance="Magelicious\Core\Model\Cache\TheCustomCache">
        <label>The Custom Cache</label>
        <description>Our custom cache type</description>
    </type>
</config>
```

Create the `<MAGELICIOUS_DIR>/Core/Model/Cache/TheCustomCache.php` file with the following content:

```
class TheCustomCache extends
\Magento\Framework\Cache\Frontend\Decorator\TagScope {
    const TYPE_IDENTIFIER = 'the_custom_cache';
    const CACHE_TAG = 'THE_CUSTOM_CACHE';

    public function
__construct(\Magento\Framework\App\Cache\Type\FrontendPool
$cacheFrontendPool) {
        parent::__construct($cacheFrontendPool->get(self::TYPE_IDENTIFIER),
self::CACHE_TAG);
    }
}
```

The `TYPE_IDENTIFIER` is used internally as a cache type code that is unique among all cache types. The `CACHE_TAG` is a cache tag that's used to distinguish the cache type from all other caches. Running `cache:status` should now show our custom cache type on the list.

We can use the instance of `Magento\Framework\App\Cache\TypeListInterface` to invalidate the cache, as follows:

```
$this->typeList->invalidate(\Magelicious\Core\Model\Cache\TheCustomCache::T
YPE_IDENTIFIER);
```

We can use the instance of `Magento\Framework\App\Cache\Manager $cacheManager` to programmatically execute the same **enable** I **disable** I **clean** operations as per the following example:

```
$cacheManager->setEnabled(
    [\Magelicious\Core\Model\Cache\TheCustomCache::TYPE_IDENTIFIER],
    true
```

```
    );

    $cacheManager->clean([\Magelicious\Core\Model\Cache\TheCustomCache::TYPE_ID
    ENTIFIER]);

    $cacheManager->flush([\Magelicious\Core\Model\Cache\TheCustomCache::TYPE_ID
    ENTIFIER]);
```

Saving data to cache requires serialization, as per the following example:

```
    // \Magento\Framework\Config\CacheInterface $cache
    // \Magento\Framework\Serialize\SerializerInterface $serializer
    // \Magento\Framework\App\Cache\StateInterface $cacheState

    $isCacheEnabled =
    $cacheState->isEnabled(\Magelicious\Core\Model\Cache\TheCustomCache::TYPE_I
    DENTIFIER);

    $cacheId = 'some-unique-identifier';

    if ($isCacheEnabled) {
        $cache->save(
            $serializer->serialize('some-data'),
            $cacheId,
            [
                \Magelicious\Core\Model\Cache\TheCustomCache::CACHE_TAG
            ]
        );
    }
```

Reading data from the cache is as easy as per the following example:

```
    if ($cacheData = $this->cache->load($cacheId);) {
        $someData = $this->getSerializer()->unserialize($cacheData);
    } else {
        $someData = $this->fetchSomeData();
    }
```

Dependency injection

Dependency injection has become a de facto standard of modern-day software. Magento makes heavy use of this technique, based on mappings found in di.xml files. The workload of Magento's dependency injection is handled by the Magento\Framework\ObjectManager\ObjectManager instance, which implements the lightweight Magento\Framework\ObjectManagerInterface.

The di.xml file configures the object manager, telling it how to handle the following:

- Argument injection
- Virtual types
- Proxies
- Factories
- Plugins

These features allow for a great degree of flexibility and extensibility, as we will soon see.

Every module can have a *global* and *area-specific* di.xml file.

Magento loads configuration files in the following order:

- Initial (app/etc/di.xml)
- Global (<ModuleDir>/etc/di.xml)
- Area-specific (<ModuleDir>/etc/<area>/di.xml)

When Magento reads all of these configuration files, it merges them all together by appending all nodes.

Argument injection

Argument injection is done via preference and type definitions within the di.xml.

By performing a lookup for the <preference string across the entire <MAGENTO_DIR> directory's di.xml files, we can see that Magento uses hundreds of preference definitions, spread across the majority of its modules.

Let's take a quick look at one of the __construct method, of the type Magento\Eav\Model\Attribute\Data\AbstractData:

```
public function __construct(
    \Magento\Framework\Stdlib\DateTime\TimezoneInterface $localeDate,
    \Psr\Log\LoggerInterface $logger,
    \Magento\Framework\Locale\ResolverInterface $localeResolver
) {
    $this->_localeDate = $localeDate;
    $this->_logger = $logger;
    $this->_localeResolver = $localeResolver;
}
```

We can find the `preference` definitions for these interfaces under the
`<MAGENTO_DIR>/magento2-base/app/etc/di.xml` file:

```
<preference for="Magento\Framework\Stdlib\DateTime\TimezoneInterface"
type="Magento\Framework\Stdlib\DateTime\Timezone" />
<preference for="Psr\Log\LoggerInterface"
type="Magento\Framework\Logger\Monolog" />
<preference for="Magento\Framework\Locale\ResolverInterface"
type="Magento\Framework\Locale\Resolver" />
```

Theoretically, we can use the object manager directly, as follows:

```
class Type {
    protected $objectManager;

    public function __construct(
        \Magento\Framework\ObjectManagerInterface $objectManager
    ) {
        $this->objectManager = $objectManager;
    }

    public function example() {
        $this->objectManager->create(\Fully\Qualified\Class\Name::class);
        $this->objectManager->get(\Fully\Qualified\Class\Name::class);
        \Magento\Framework\App\ObjectManager::getInstance()
            ->create(\Fully\Qualified\Class\Name::class);
        \Magento\Framework\App\ObjectManager::getInstance()
            ->get(\Fully\Qualified\Class\Name::class);
    }
}
```

The direct use of the `objectManager` is highly discouraged, as it prevents
type validation and type hinting that a factory class provides.

By doing a lookup for the `<type` string across the entire `<MAGENTO_DIR>` directory's
`di.xml` files, we can see that Magento uses over a thousand type definitions, spread across
the majority of its modules.

Here is a very simple example, taken from the `<MAGENTO_DIR>/module-
customer/etc/di.xml` file:

```
<type name="Magento\Customer\Model\Visitor">
    <arguments>
        <argument name="ignoredUserAgents" xsi:type="array">
            <item name="google1" xsi:type="string">Googlebot/1.0
```

```
(googlebot@googlebot.com http://googlebot.com/)</item>
            <item name="google2" xsi:type="string">Mozilla/5.0 (compatible;
Googlebot/2.1; +http://www.google.com/bot.html)</item>
            <item name="google3" xsi:type="string">Googlebot/2.1
(+http://www.googlebot.com/bot.html)</item>
        </argument>
    </arguments>
</type>
```

Looking into the source of the `Magento\Customer\Model\Visitor` class, we can see that it has its constructor defined by the `$ignoredUserAgents = []` array. Using the `type` element, the preceding example injects the `ignoredUserAgents` argument with the given array values.

When configuration files for a given scope get merged, array arguments with the same name get merged into a new array. However, if any new configuration is loaded at a later time, either by a more specific scope or through the code, then any array definitions in the new configuration will replace the loaded configuration instead of merging.

The list of available item type values goes well beyond just a string, and includes the following:

- `boolean`
- `string`
- `number`
- `null`
- `object`
- `const`
- `init_parameter`
- `array`

 See `<MAGENTO_DIR>/framework/Data/etc/argument/types.xsd` and `<MAGENTO_DIR>/framework/ObjectManager/etc/config.xsd` for specific type definitions.

Argument injection often goes hand in hand with *virtual types*, as we will soon see.

Virtual types

Virtual types are a very neat feature of Magento that allow us to change the arguments of a specific injectable dependency and thus change the behavior of a particular class type.

The `<MAGENTO_DIR>/module-checkout/etc/di.xml` file provides a simple example of `virtualType` and its usage:

```
<virtualType name="Magento\Checkout\Model\Session\Storage"
type="Magento\Framework\Session\Storage">
    <arguments>
        <argument name="namespace" xsi:type="string">checkout</argument>
    </arguments>
</virtualType>
<type name="Magento\Checkout\Model\Session">
    <arguments>
        <argument name="storage"
xsi:type="object">Magento\Checkout\Model\Session\Storage</argument>
    </arguments>
</type>
```

The `virtualType` here (virtually) extends `Magento\Framework\Session\Storage` by rewriting its constructor's `$namespace = 'default'` argument to `$namespace = 'checkout'`. However, this change does not kick in on its own, as the `Magento\Checkout\Model\Session\Storage` virtual type *must be used* first. It is used in this case, via a `type` definition, where the storage argument is replaced entirely by the virtual type.

 Most of the `virtualType` name attributes across Magento take the form of a non-existing fully qualified class name, though this can be any character combination that's allowed in PHP array keys.

By doing a lookup for the `<virtualType` string across the entire `<MAGENTO_DIR>` directory's `di.xml` files, we can see that Magento *uses hundreds* of virtual types across the majority of its modules.

A more complex example of virtual type usage can be found under the `Magento_LayeredNavigation` module.

The `<MAGENTO_DIR>/module-layered-navigation/etc/frontend/di.xml` file defines two virtual types, as follows:

```
<virtualType name="Magento\LayeredNavigation\Block\Navigation\Category"
type="Magento\LayeredNavigation\Block\Navigation">
    <arguments>
        <argument name="filterList"
xsi:type="object">categoryFilterList</argument>
    </arguments>
</virtualType>

<virtualType name="Magento\LayeredNavigation\Block\Navigation\Search"
type="Magento\LayeredNavigation\Block\Navigation">
    <arguments>
        <argument name="filterList"
xsi:type="object">searchFilterList</argument>
    </arguments>
</virtualType>
```

Here, we have two virtual types defined, each changing the `filterList` argument of the `Magento\LayeredNavigation\Block\Navigation` class. `categoryFilterList` and `searchFilterList` are the names of two other virtual types that are defined in `<MAGENTO_DIR>/module-catalog-search/etc/di.xml`, as visible here: https://github.com/magento/magento2/blob/2.2/app/code/Magento/CatalogSearch/etc/di.xml.

The `Magento\LayeredNavigation\Block\Navigation\Category` and `Magento\LayeredNavigation\Block\Navigation\Search` virtual types are then used in layout files for block definition, as follows:

```
<!-- view/frontend/layout/catalog_category_view_type_layered.xml -->
<referenceContainer name="sidebar.main">
    <block class="Magento\LayeredNavigation\Block\Navigation\Category" ...
</referenceContainer>

<!-- view/frontend/layout/catalogsearch_result_index.xml -->
<referenceContainer name="sidebar.main">
    <block class="Magento\LayeredNavigation\Block\Navigation\Search" ...
</referenceContainer>
```

What this effectively does is tell Magento that, for the category view page and search page, use the virtual type for class, thus instructing it to go through all the argument changes specified in the virtual type.

This is an interesting example as it reveals the potential complexity of using virtual types. Basically, we have one virtual type (`Magento\LayeredNavigation\Block\Navigation\Search`) changing the single `filterList` argument of a real type (`Magento\LayeredNavigation\Block\Navigation`) with another virtual type (`categoryFilterList`). Likewise, we just learned how the class property of the block element is capable of not just accepting the fully qualified class name, but the `virtualType` name as well.

Proxies

Proxy classes are used when object creation is *expensive* and a class' constructor is unusually *resource-intensive*. To avoid unnecessary performance impact, Magento uses Proxy classes to turn given types into becoming lazy-loaded versions of them.

A quick lookup for the `\Proxy</argument>` string across all Magento `di.xml` files reveals over a hundred occurrences of this string. It goes to say that Magento extensively uses proxies across its code.

The type definition under `<MAGENTO_DIR>/module-customer/etc/di.xml` is a nice example of using proxies:

```
<type name="Magento\Customer\Model\Session">
    <arguments>
        <argument name="configShare"
xsi:type="object">Magento\Customer\Model\Config\Share\Proxy</argument>
        <argument name="customerUrl"
xsi:type="object">Magento\Customer\Model\Url\Proxy</argument>
        <argument name="customerResource"
xsi:type="object">Magento\Customer\Model\ResourceModel\Customer\Proxy</argu
ment>
        <argument name="storage"
xsi:type="object">Magento\Customer\Model\Session\Storage</argument>
        <argument name="customerRepository"
xsi:type="object">Magento\Customer\Api\CustomerRepositoryInterface\Proxy</a
rgument>
    </arguments>
</type>
```

If we look at the constructor of the Magento\Customer\Model\Session type, we can see that none of the four arguments (configShare, customerUrl, customerResource, and customerRepository) were declared as Proxy within the PHP file. They where rewritten through di.xml. These Proxy types do not really exist just yet, as the Magento **dependency injection (di)** compilation process creates them. They are automatically generated under the generated directory.

Once it is compiled, the Magento\Customer\Model\Url\Proxy type can easily be found under the generated/code/Magento/Customer/Model/Url/Proxy.php file. Let's take a partial look at it:

```
class Proxy extends \Magento\Customer\Model\Url
implements \Magento\Framework\ObjectManager\NonInterceptableInterface {
    public function __construct(
        \Magento\Framework\ObjectManagerInterface $objectManager,
        $instanceName = '\\Magento\\Customer\\Model\\Url',
        $shared = true) {
        $this->_objectManager = $objectManager;
        $this->_instanceName = $instanceName;
        $this->_isShared = $shared;
    }

    public function __sleep() {
        return ['_subject', '_isShared', '_instanceName'];
    }

    public function __wakeup() {
        $this->_objectManager =
\Magento\Framework\App\ObjectManager::getInstance();
    }

    public function __clone() {
        $this->_subject = clone $this->_getSubject();
    }

    protected function _getSubject() {
        if (!$this->_subject) {
            $this->_subject = true === $this->_isShared
                ? $this->_objectManager->get($this->_instanceName)
                : $this->_objectManager->create($this->_instanceName);
        }
        return $this->_subject;
    }

    public function getLoginUrl() {
        return $this->_getSubject()->getLoginUrl();
```

```
    }

    public function getLoginUrlParams() {
        return $this->_getSubject()->getLoginUrlParams();
    }
}
```

The composition of the `Proxy` class shows the mechanism by which it wraps around the original `Magento\Customer\Model\Url` type. This now means that, across Magento, every time the `Magento\Customer\Model\Url` type is requested, the `Magento\Customer\Model\Url\Proxy` is going to get passed instead. Unlike the original type's `__construct` method which might be performance heavy, the autogenerated Proxy's `__construct` method is a lightweight one. This eliminates possible performance bottlenecks. The `_getSubject` method is used to instantiate/lazy load the original type whenever any of the original type public methods are called. For example, the call to the `getLoginUrl` method would go through the proxy.

Every proxy generated by Magento implements `Magento\Framework\ObjectManager\NoninterceptableInterface`. Though the interface itself is empty, it is used as a marker to identify proxies for which we don't need to generate interceptors (plugins).

When writing custom types, such as `Magelicious\Core\Model\Customer`, we could easily specify the proxy right there in the constructor:

```
class Customer {
    public function __construct(
        \Magento\Customer\Model\Url\Proxy $customerUrl
    ) {
        //...
    }
}
```

This approach, however, is a *bad practice*. The way to do this properly is to specify `__construct` with an original `Magento\Customer\Model\Url` type and then add the `di.xml` as follows:

```
<type name="Magelicious\Core\Model\Customer">
    <arguments>
        <argument name="customerUrl"
xsi:type="object">Magento\Customer\Model\Url\Proxy</argument>
    </arguments>
</type>
```

Factories

Factories are classes that create other classes—much like the object manager, except this time we are encouraged to use them directly. Their purpose is to instantiate the non-injectable classes—those that we should not inject directly into __construct. The beauty of using factories is that, most of the time, we don't even have to write them, as they are automatically generated by Magento unless we need to implement some sort of specific behavior for our factory classes.

By doing a lookup for the Factory $ string across the entire <MAGENTO_DIR> directory's *.php files, we can see thousands of factory examples, spread across the majority of Magento's modules.

While a great deal of these factories actually exist, others are automatically generated when needed.

Let's take a quick look at one automatically generated factory, that of Magento\Newsletter\Model\SubscriberFactory, which is used in several Magento modules such as the newsletter, subscriber, and review modules:

```
class SubscriberFactory {
    protected $_objectManager = null;
    protected $_instanceName = null;

    public function __construct(
        \Magento\Framework\ObjectManagerInterface $objectManager,
        $instanceName = '\\Magento\\Newsletter\\Model\\Subscriber'
    ) {
        $this->_objectManager = $objectManager;
        $this->_instanceName = $instanceName;
    }

    public function create(array $data = array()) {
        return $this->_objectManager->create($this->_instanceName, $data);
    }
}
```

The autogenerated factory code is essentially just a thin wrapper on top of an object manager create method.

Factories work well with the di.xml preference mechanism, which means we can easily pass interfaces into the constructor, like so:

```
public function __construct(
    \Magento\CatalogInventory\Api\StockItemRepositoryInterface
$stockItemRepository,
```

```
        \Magento\CatalogInventory\Api\StockItemCriteriaInterfaceFactory
    $stockItemCriteriaFactory
    ) {
        $this->stockItemRepository = $stockItemRepository;
        $this->stockItemCriteriaFactory = $stockItemCriteriaFactory;
    }

    // $criteria = $this->stockItemCriteriaFactory->create();
    // $result = $this->stockItemRepository->getList($criteria);
```

The preference mechanism makes sure that concrete implementations get passed to the object instance when its constructor is invoked.

> While in developer mode, Magento performs automatic compilation, meaning that changes to di.xml are automatically picked up. Sometimes, however, if we stumble upon unexpected results, running the bin/magento setup:di:compile console command or even manually clearing the generated folder (rm -rf generated/*) might help sort out the issues.

Plugins

Plugins are likely one of the most powerful features of Magento. They allow us to modify the behavior of public class functions by intercepting a function call and running code *before*, *after*, or *around* that function call.

Before we eagerly start using them, it is worth emphasizing how plugins *can't be used* on the following:

- Final methods
- Final classes
- Non-public methods
- Class methods (such as static methods)
- __construct
- Virtual types
- Objects that are instantiated before Magento or Framework\Interception is bootstrapped

Plugins *can be used* on the following:

- Classes
- Interfaces
- Abstract classes
- Parent classes

By doing a lookup for the `<plugin` string across the entire `<MAGENTO_DIR>` directory's `di.xml` files, we can see hundreds of plugin examples spread across the majority of Magento's modules.

The before plugin

The `before` plugin, as its name suggests, runs before the observed method.

When writing a `before` plugin, there are a few key points to remember:

1. The `before` keyword is appended to *the observed* instance method. If the observed method is called `getSomeValue`, then the plugin method is called `beforeGetSomeValue`.
2. The first parameter of the *before* plugin method is always the observed instance type, often abbreviated as `$subject` or directly by the class type – which is `$processor` in our example. We can typecast it for greater readability.
3. All other parameters of the plugin method must match the parameters of the observed method.
4. The plugin method must return an array with the same type and number of parameters as the observed method's input parameters.

Let's take a look at one of Magento's *before* plugin implementations, the one specified in the `<MAGENTO_DIR>module-payment/etc/frontend/di.xml` file:

```
<type name="Magento\Checkout\Block\Checkout\LayoutProcessor">
    <plugin name="ProcessPaymentConfiguration"
            type="Magento\Payment\Plugin\PaymentConfigurationProcess"/>
</type>
```

The original method this plugin is targeting is the `process` method of the `Magento\Checkout\Block\Checkout\LayoutProcessor` class:

```
public function process($jsLayout) {
    // The rest of the code...
    return $jsLayout;
}
```

The implementation of the `before` plugin is provided via the `beforeProcess` method of the `Magento\Payment\Plugin\PaymentConfigurationProcess` class, as per the following partial example:

```
public function beforeProcess(
    \Magento\Checkout\Block\Checkout\LayoutProcessor $processor,
    $jsLayout) {
    // The rest of the code...
    return [$jsLayout];
}
```

The around plugin

The `around` plugin runs around the observed method in a way that allows us to run some code before and after the original method call. This is a very powerful concept, as we get to change the incoming parameters as well as the return value of a function.

When writing the `around` plugin, there are a few key points to remember:

1. The first parameter coming into the plugin is the observed type instance.
2. The second parameter coming into the plugin is a callable/Closure. Usually, this parameter is typed and named as `callable $proceed`. We must make sure to forward the same parameters to this callable as the original method signature.
3. All other parameters are parameters of the original observed method.
4. The plugin must return the same value as the original function, ideally `return $proceed(...)` or `$returnValue = $proceed();` followed by `$returnValue;` for cases where we need to modify the `$returnValue`.

Let's take a look at one of Magento's `around` plugin implementations, the one specified in the `<MAGENTO_DIR>module-grouped-product/etc/di.xml` file:

```
<type name="Magento\Catalog\Model\ResourceModel\Product\Link">
    <plugin name="groupedProductLinkProcessor"
type="Magento\GroupedProduct\Model\ResourceModel\Product\Link\RelationPersi
ster" />
</type>
```

The original method of this plugin is *targeting* the `deleteProductLink` method of the `Magento\Catalog\Model\ResourceModel\Product\Link` class:

```
public function deleteProductLink($linkId) {
    return $this->getConnection()
            ->delete($this->getMainTable(), ['link_id = ?' => $linkId]);
}
```

The implementation of the `around` plugin is provided via the `aroundDeleteProductLink` method of the `Magento\GroupedProduct\Model\ResourceModel\Product\Link\RelationPersist` er class, as per the following partial example:

```
public function aroundDeleteProductLink(
    \Magento\GroupedProduct\Model\ResourceModel\Product\Link $subject,
    \Closure $proceed, $linkId) {
    // The rest of the code...
    $result = $proceed($linkId);
    // The rest of the code...
    return $result;
}
```

The after plugin

The `after` plugin, as its name suggests, runs after the observed method.

When writing the `after` plugin, there are a few key points to remember:

1. The first parameter coming into the plugin is an observed type instance.
2. The second parameter coming into the plugin is the result of the observed method, often called `$result` or called after the variable returned from the observed method (as in the following example: `$data`).
3. All other parameters are parameters of the observed method.
4. The plugin must return the same `$result` | `$data` variable of the same type, as we are free to modify the value.

Let's take a look at one of Magento's `after` plugin implementations, the one specified in the `module-catalog/etc/di.xml` file:

```
<type name="Magento\Indexer\Model\Config\Data">
    <plugin name="indexerProductFlatConfigGet"
type="Magento\Catalog\Model\Indexer\Product\Flat\Plugin\IndexerConfigData"
/>
</type>
```

The original method this plugin is *targeting* is the `get` method of the `Magento\Indexer\Model\Config\Data` class:

```
public function get($path = null, $default = null) {
    // The rest of the code...
    return $data;
}
```

The implementation of the `after` plugin is provided via the `afterGet` method of the `Magento\Catalog\Model\Indexer\Product\Flat\Plugin\IndexerConfigData` class, as per the following partial example:

```
public function afterGet(Magento\Indexer\Model\Config\Data, $data, $path =
null, $default = null) {
    // The rest of the code...
    return $data;
}
```

Special care should be taken when using plugins. While they provide great flexibility, they also make it easy to induce bugs, performance bottlenecks, and other less obvious types of instabilities – even more so if several plugins are observing the same method.

Events and observers

Magento has a neat publish-subscribe pattern implementation that we call events and observers. By dispatching events when certain actions are triggered, we can run our custom code in response to the triggered event. The events are dispatched using the `Magento\Framework\Event\Manager` class, which implements `Magento\Framework\Event\ManagerInterface`.

To dispatch an event, we simply call the dispatch method of the event manager instance, providing it with the name of the event we are dispatching with an optional array of data we wish to pass on to the observers, as per the following example taken from the `<MAGENTO_DIR>/module-customer/Controller/Account/CreatePost.php` file:

```
$this->_eventManager->dispatch(
    'customer_register_success',
    ['account_controller' => $this, 'customer' => $customer]
);
```

Observers are registered via an events.xml file, as per the following example from the `<MAGENTO_DIR>/module-persistent/etc/frontend/events.xml` file:

```
<event name="customer_register_success">
  <observer name="persistent"
instance="Magento\Persistent\Observer\RemovePersistentCookieOnRegisterObser
ver" />
</event>
```

By doing a lookup for the eventManager->dispatch string across the entire `<MAGENTO_DIR>` directory's *.php files, we can see hundreds of events examples, spread across the majority of Magento's modules. While all of these events are of the same technical importance, we might say that some are likely to be used more on a day to day basis than others.

This makes it worth taking some time to study the following classes and the events they dispatch:

- The Magento\Framework\App\Action\Action class, with the following events:
    - controller_action_predispatch
    - 'controller_action_predispatch_' . $request->getRouteName()
    - 'controller_action_predispatch_' . $request->getFullActionName()
    - 'controller_action_postdispatch_' . $request->getFullActionName()
    - 'controller_action_postdispatch_' . $request->getRouteName()
    - controller_action_postdispatch

- The `Magento\Framework\Model\AbstractModel` class, with the following events:
    - `model_load_before`
    - `$this->_eventPrefix . '_load_before'`
    - `model_load_after`
    - `$this->_eventPrefix . '_load_after'`
    - `model_save_commit_after`
    - `$this->_eventPrefix . '_save_commit_after'`
    - `model_save_before`
    - `$this->_eventPrefix . '_save_before'`
    - `model_save_after`
    - `clean_cache_by_tags`
    - `$this->_eventPrefix . '_save_after'`
    - `model_delete_before`
    - `$this->_eventPrefix . '_delete_before'`
    - `model_delete_after`
    - `clean_cache_by_tags`
    - `$this->_eventPrefix . '_delete_after'`
    - `model_delete_commit_after`
    - `$this->_eventPrefix . '_delete_commit_after'`
    - `$this->_eventPrefix . '_clear'`
- The `Magento\Framework\Model\ResourceModel\Db\Collection` class, with the following events:
    - `core_collection_abstract_load_before`
    - `$this->_eventPrefix . '_load_before'`
    - `core_collection_abstract_load_after`
    - `$this->_eventPrefix . '_load_after'`

Some more important events can be found in a few of the types defined under the `<MAGENTO_DIR>/framework/View` directory:

- `view_block_abstract_to_html_before`
- `view_block_abstract_to_html_after`
- `view_message_block_render_grouped_html_after`
- `layout_render_before`

- `'layout_render_before_' . $this->request->getFullActionName()`
- `core_layout_block_create_after`
- `layout_load_before`
- `layout_generate_blocks_before`
- `layout_generate_blocks_after`
- `core_layout_render_element`

Let's take a closer look at one of these events, the one found in the `<MAGENTO_DIR>/framework/Model/AbstractModel.php` file:

```
public function afterCommitCallback() {
    $this->_eventManager->dispatch('model_save_commit_after', ['object' =>
$this]);
    $this->_eventManager->dispatch($this->_eventPrefix .
'_save_commit_after', $this->_getEventData());
    return $this;
}

protected function _getEventData() {
    return [
        'data_object' => $this,
        $this->_eventObject => $this,
    ];
}
```

The `$_eventPrefix` and `$_eventObject` type properties are particularly important here. If we glimpse over types such as `Magento\Catalog\Model\Product`, `Magento\Catalog\Model\Category`, `Magento\Customer\Model\Customer`, `Magento\Quote\Model\Quote`, `Magento\Sales\Model\Order`, and others, we can see that a great deal of these entity types are essentially extending from `Magento\Framework\Model\AbstractModel` and provide their own values to replace `$_eventPrefix = 'core_abstract'` and `$_eventObject = 'object'`. What this means is that we can use events such as `$this->_eventPrefix . '_save_commit_after'` to specify observers via `events.xml`.

Let's take a look at the following example, taken from the `<MAGENTO_DIR>/module-downloadable/etc/events.xml` file:

```
<config>
    <event name="sales_order_save_commit_after">
        <observer name="downloadable_observer"
instance="Magento\Downloadable\Observer\SetLinkStatusObserver" />
    </event>
</config>
```

Observers are placed inside the `<ModuleDir>/Observer` directory. Every observer implements a single `execute` method on the `Magento\Framework\Event\ObserverInterface` class:

```
class SetLinkStatusObserver implements
\Magento\Framework\Event\ObserverInterface {
    public function execute(\Magento\Framework\Event\Observer $observer) {
        $order = $observer->getEvent()->getOrder();
    }
}
```

Much like plugins, badly implemented observers can easily cause bugs or even break the entire application. This is why we need to keep our observer small and computationally efficient—to avoid performance bottlenecks.

The *cyclical event loop* is a trap that's easy to fall into. This happens when an observer, at some point, is dispatching the same event that it listens to. For example, if an observer listens to the `model_save_before` event, and then tries to save the same entity again within the observer, this would trigger a cyclical event loop.

To make our observers as specific as possible, we need to declare them in an appropriate scope:

- For observing frontend only events, you can declare observers in `<ModuleDir>/etc/frontend/events.xml`
- For observing backend only events, you can declare observers in `<ModuleDir>/etc/adminhtml/events.xml`
- For observing global events, you can declare observers in `<ModuleDir>/etc/events.xml`

Unlike plugins, observers are used for triggering the *follow-up* functionality, rather than changing the behavior of functions or data which is part of the event they are observing.

Console commands

The built-in `bin/magento` tool plays a major role – not just in Magento development, but in production deployments as well.

Right out of the box, it provides a dozen commands that we can use to manage caches, indexers, dependency compilation, deploying static view files, creating CSS from LESS, putting our store to maintenance, installing modules, and more.

Quite easily, Magento enables us to add our own commands to its Symfony-like command-line interface (CLI). The Magento CLI essentially extends from `Symfony\Component\Console\Command`.

The real value in creating our own command lies in the arguments and options that we can make available, thus passing dynamic information to the command.

Magento console commands reside under the `<ModuleName>/Console` directory, which can further be organized to better accommodate our commands. Magento mostly uses the `<ModuleName>/Console/Command` directory to place the actual CLI command class, whereas various options and other accompanying classes reside in the `<ModuleName>/Console` directory.

Conceptually, creating a new CLI command is as easy as doing the following:

1. Creating the command class
2. Wiring it up via `di.xml`
3. Clearing the cache and compiled directories

Let's create our own simple console command. We will start off by creating the `<MAGELICIOUS_DIR>/Core/Console/Command/RunStockImportCommand.php` file with the following content:

```php
use Symfony\Component\Console\Command\Command;
use Symfony\Component\Console\Input\InputArgument;
use Symfony\Component\Console\Input\InputOption;
use Symfony\Component\Console\Input\InputInterface;
use Symfony\Component\Console\Output\OutputInterface;

class RunStockImportCommand extends Command {
    const ORDER_ID_ARGUMENT = 'order_id';
    const DAYS_BACK_OPTION = 'days_back';

    protected function configure() {
        $this->setName('magelicious:stock:import')
            ->setDescription('The Magelicious Stock Import.')
            ->setDefinition([
                new InputArgument(
                    self::ORDER_ID_ARGUMENT, /* name */
                    InputArgument::REQUIRED, /* mode REQUIRED or OPTIONAL */
                    'The argument to set.', /* description */
                    null /* default */
                ),
                new InputOption(
```

```
                    self::DAYS_BACK_OPTION, /* name */
                    null, /* shortcut */
                    InputOption::VALUE_OPTIONAL, /* VALUE_NONE or
VALUE_REQUIRED or VALUE_OPTIONAL or VALUE_IS_ARRAY */
                    'The option to set.' /* description */
                )
            ]);
        parent::configure();
    }

    protected function execute(InputInterface $input, OutputInterface
$output) {
        try {
            $output->setDecorated(true);
            // $input->getArgument(self::ORDER_ID_ARGUMENT);
            // $input->getOption(self::DAYS_BACK_OPTION);
            // green text
            $output->writeln('<info>The info message.</info>');
            // yellow text
            $output->writeln('<comment>The comment message.</comment>');
            // black text on a cyan background
            $output->writeln('<question>The question message.</question>');
            return \Magento\Framework\Console\Cli::RETURN_SUCCESS;
        } catch (\Exception $e) {
            // white text on a red background
            $output->writeln('<error>' . $e->getMessage() . '</error>');
            if ($output->getVerbosity() >=
OutputInterface::VERBOSITY_VERBOSE) {
                $output->writeln($e->getTraceAsString());
            }
            return \Magento\Framework\Console\Cli::RETURN_FAILURE;
        }
    }
}
```

We then wire it up via `<MAGELICIOUS_DIR>/etc/di.xml`, as follows:

```
<type name="Magento\Framework\Console\CommandListInterface">
    <arguments>
        <argument name="commands" xsi:type="array">
            <item name="runStockImport"
xsi:type="object">Magelicious\Core\Console\Command\RunStockImportCommand</item>
        </argument>
    </arguments>
</type>
```

We can now clear the cache and the compiled directories either by running the `php bin/magento cache:clean` config followed by `php bin/magento setup:di:compile`, or by running `rm -rf generated/*` and `rm -rf var/cache/*`.

Now, if we run the `php bin/magento` command, we should see our command on the list:

```
magelicious
  magelicious:stock:import The Magelicious Stock Import.
```

If we now test our method by running `php bin/magento magelicious:stock:import`, this should immediately trigger an error, as follows:

```
[Symfony\Component\Console\Exception\RuntimeException]
Not enough arguments (missing: "order_id").

magelicious:stock:import [--days_back [DAYS_BACK]] [--] <order_id>
```

Either of the following calls should work:

```
php bin/magento magelicious:stock:import 000000060
php bin/magento magelicious:stock:import 000000060 --days_back=7
```

Cron jobs

Creating a new cron job is as easy as doing the following:

1. Creating a job definition under the `<ModuleName>/etc/crontab.xml` file
2. Creating a class with a public method that handles the job execution

Let's create a simple cron job. We will start off by creating the `<MAGELICIOUS_DIR>/Core/etc/crontab.xml` file with the following content:

```
<group id="default">
    <job name="the_job" instance="Magelicious\Core\Cron\TheJob"
method="execute">
        <schedule>*/15 * * * *</schedule>
    </job>
</group>
```

The instance and method values map to the class and method within that class, which will be executed when cron job is run. The schedule is a cron, like the expression for when the job is to be executed. Unless there are specific requirements telling us otherwise, we can safely use the `default` group.

We then create the <MAGELICIOUS_DIR>/Core/Cron/TheJob.php file with the following content:

```
class TheJob {
    public function execute() {
        // ...
    }
}
```

The Magento console command supports several console commands:

```
cron
  cron:install Generates and installs crontab for current user
  cron:remove Removes tasks from crontab
  cron:run Runs jobs by schedule
```

To get our cron job running, we need to make sure that crontab is installed, by running php bin/magento cron:install. This command generates and installs crontab for the current user. We can confirm that by following up with the crontab -e command, like so:

```
#~ MAGENTO START 6f7c468a10aea2972eab1da53c8d2fce
* * * * * /bin/php /magelicious/bin/magento cron:run 2>&1 | grep -v "Ran
jobs by schedule" >> /magelicious/var/log/magento.cron.log
* * * * * /bin/php /magelicious/update/cron.php >>
/magelicious/var/log/update.cron.log
* * * * * /bin/php /magelicious/bin/magento setup:cron:run >>
/magelicious/var/log/setup.cron.log
#~ MAGENTO END 6f7c468a10aea2972eab1da53c8d2fce
```

Now, if we execute php bin/magento cron:run, the_job should find its way under the cron_schedule table.

 Depending on the schedule_generate_every and schedule_ahead_for options for a particular cron group, we might not see some cron jobs instantly showing up in the cron_schedule table.

Magento Open Source provides two cron groups: default and index. While the majority of times our cron jobs will be placed under the default group, there might be a need to create a completely new cron group. Luckily, this is quite easy.

To create a new cron group, all we need is a
`<MAGELICIOUS_DIR>/etc/cron_groups.xml` file with the following content:

```
<config>
    <group id="magelicious">
        <schedule_generate_every>15</schedule_generate_every>
        <schedule_ahead_for>20</schedule_ahead_for>
        <schedule_lifetime>15</schedule_lifetime>
        <history_cleanup_every>10</history_cleanup_every>
        <history_success_lifetime>10080</history_success_lifetime>
        <history_failure_lifetime>10080</history_failure_lifetime>
        <use_separate_process>0</use_separate_process>
    </group>
</config>
```

While group information is not stored in the `cron_schedule` table, we can use it via the Magento CLI to run jobs that are specific to a certain group:

```
php bin/magento cron:run --group=default
```

Summary

In this chapter, we touched upon some of Magento's keys components. Plugins and event observers provide a powerful way of extending Magento, either by changing the behavior of existing functions or by running some *follow-up* code in response to certain events.

Moving forward, we will deepen our Magento knowledge further by looking into the install and update scripts, the **Entity–Attribute–Value** model (**EAV**), creating new EAV types, indexers, extension, and custom attributes.

2
Working with Entities

Every Magento module hosts its *models* within the `Models` directory. Some of these models are *persistable*, while others are *non-persistable*. A great deal of custom, third-party, and core Magento modules persist data to the database. Data persistence is one of the key functionalities that platforms like Magento need to deal with. Terminology-wise, Magento uses terms such as *model, resource model,* and *collection* for a group of three classes that deal with data persistence, that is, **create, read, update,** and **delete** (**CRUD**) operations.

To better understand the overall mechanism of entities, we are going to take a closer look at the following:

- Understanding types of models:
  - Creating a simple model
  - Methods worth memorizing
- Working with setup scripts:
  - The `InstallSchema` script
  - The `UpgradeSchema` script
  - The `Recurring` script
  - The `InstallData` script
  - The `UpgradeData` script
  - The `RecurringData` script
- Creating extension attributes

Technical requirements

You will need to have basic knowledge of PHP, OOP, JavaScript, and XML. You will also need Apache, MySQL, and AMPPS installed on your system to execute the codes.

The code files of this chapter can be found on GitHub:
`https://github.com/PacktPublishing/Magento-2-Quick-Start-Guide.`

Check out the following video to see the Code in Action:

```
http://bit.ly/2PKYvUx.
```

Understanding types of models

There are two types of persistence models in Magento: **simple** and **Entity–attribute–value** (**EAV**). The term *entity* is tossed around interchangeably between the two types of models. We can think of an entity as any persistable model.

The `Subscriber` entity of the `Magento_Newsletter` module is an example of a simple model. We can see that it's comprised of the following:

- A model of type `Magento\Newsletter\Model\Subscriber` extends `Magento\Framework\Model\AbstractModel`
- A resource model of type `Magento\Newsletter\Model\ResourceModel\Subscriber` extends `Magento\Framework\Model\ResourceModel\Db\AbstractDb`
- A collection of type `Magento\Newsletter\Model\ResourceModel\Subscriber\Collection` extends `Magento\Framework\Model\ResourceModel\Db\Collection\AbstractCollection`

The `Customer` entity of the `Magento_Customer` module is an example of an EAV model. We can see that it's comprised of the following:

- A model of type `Magento\Customer\Model\Customer` extends `Magento\Framework\Model\AbstractModel`
- A resource model of type `Magento\Customer\Model\ResourceModel\Customer` extends `Magento\Eav\Model\Entity\VersionControl\AbstractEntity`
- A collection of type `Magento\Customer\Model\ResourceModel\Customer\Collection` extends `Magento\Eav\Model\Entity\Collection\VersionControl\AbstractCollection`

What differentiates EAV from simple models is essentially their *resource model* and *collection* classes. The resource model is our *link* to the database—our *persistor*, if you will.

When a subscriber is saved, its data gets saved *horizontally* in the database. Data from the subscriber model gets dumped into the single `newsletter_subscriber` table.

When a customer is saved, its data gets saved *vertically* in the database. Data from the customer model gets dumped into the following tables:

- `customer_entity`
- `customer_entity_datetime`
- `customer_entity_decimal`
- `customer_entity_int`
- `customer_entity_text`
- `customer_entity_varchar`

The decision as to where to store a value for an individual attribute is contained in the `eav_attribute.backend_type` column. The `SELECT DISTINCT backend_type FROM eav_attribute;` query reveals the following:

- The `static` attribute value gets stored in the `<entityName>_entity` table
- The `varchar` attribute value gets stored in the `<entityName>_entity_varchar` table
- The `int` attribute value gets stored in the `<entityName>_entity_int` table
- The `text` attribute value gets stored in the `<entityName>_entity_text` table
- The `datetime` attribute value gets stored in the `<entityName>_entity_datetime` table
- The `decimal` attribute value gets stored in the `<entityName>_entity_decimal` table

Next to the `eav_attribute` table, the remaining relevant information is scattered around the dozen of other `eav_*` tables, the most important being the `eav_attribute_*` tables:

- `eav_attribute`
- `eav_attribute_group`
- `eav_attribute_label`
- `eav_attribute_option`
- `eav_attribute_option_swatch`
- `eav_attribute_option_value`
- `eav_attribute_set`

The `SELECT entity_type_code, entity_model FROM eav_entity_type;` query indicates that the following Magento entities are from an EAV model:

- `customer: Magento\Customer\Model\ResourceModel\Customer`
- `customer_address: Magento\Customer\Model\ResourceModel\Address`
- `catalog_category: Magento\Catalog\Model\ResourceModel\Category`
- `catalog_product: Magento\Catalog\Model\ResourceModel\Product`
- `order: Magento\Sales\Model\ResourceModel\Order`
- `invoice: Magento\Sales\Model\ResourceModel\Order\Invoice`
- `creditmemo: Magento\Sales\Model\ResourceModel\Order\Creditmemo`
- `shipment: Magento\Sales\Model\ResourceModel\Order\Shipment`

However, not all of them use the EAV model to its full extent, as indicated by the `SELECT DISTINCT entity_type_id FROM eav_attribute;` query, which points only to the following:

- `customer`
- `customer_address`
- `catalog_category`
- `catalog_product`

What this means is that only four models in Magento Open Source really use EAV models for managing their attributes and storing data vertically through EAV tables. The rest are all *flat* tables, as all attributes and their values are in a single table.

The EAV models are inherently more complex to work with. They come in handy for cases where dynamic attribute creation is needed, ideally via an admin interface, as is the case with products. The majority of the time, however, simple models will do the job.

Creating a simple model

Unlike EAV models, creating simple models is pretty straightforward. Let's go ahead and create a model, resource model, and a collection for a `Log` entity.

We will start off by creating the `<MAGELICIOUS_DIR>/Core/Model/Log.php` file with the following content:

```
class Log extends \Magento\Framework\Model\AbstractModel {
    protected $_eventPrefix = 'magelicious_core_log';
    protected $_eventObject = 'log';
```

```
    protected function _construct() {
        $this->_init(\Magelicious\Core\Model\ResourceModel\Log::class);
    }
}
```

The use of $_eventPrefix and $_eventObject is not mandatory, but it is *highly recommended*. These values are used by the Magento\Framework\Model\AbstractModel event dispatcher and add to the future extensibility of our module. While Magento uses the <ModuleName>_<ModelName> convention for $_eventPrefix naming, we might be safer using <VendorName>_<ModuleName>_<ModelName>. The $_eventObject, by convention, usually bears the name of the model itself.

We then create the <MAGELICIOUS_DIR>/Core/Model/ResourceModel/Log.php file with the following content:

```
class Log extends \Magento\Framework\Model\ResourceModel\Db\AbstractDb {
    protected function _construct() {
        $this->_init('magelicious_core_log', 'entity_id');
    }
}
```

The _init method here takes two arguments: the magelicious_core_log value for the $mainTable argument and the entity_id value for the $idFieldName argument. The $idFieldName is the name of the primary column in the designated database. It's worth noting that the magelicious_core_log table still doesn't exist, but we will address that in a bit.

We will then create the <MAGELICIOUS_DIR>/Core/Model/ResourceModel/Log/Collection.php file with the following content:

```
class Collection extends
\Magento\Framework\Model\ResourceModel\Db\Collection\AbstractCollection {
    protected function _construct() {
        $this->_init(
            \Magelicious\Core\Model\Log::class,
            \Magelicious\Core\Model\ResourceModel\Log::class
        );
    }
}
```

The _init method here takes two arguments: the string names of $model and $resourceModel. Magento uses the <FULLY_QUALIFIED_CLASS_NAME>::class syntax for this, as it uses a nifty solution instead of passing class strings around.

Methods worth memorizing

Both EAV and simple models extend from
the `Magento\Framework\Model\AbstractModel` class, which further extends from
`Magento\Framework\DataObject`. The `DataObject` has some neat methods worth
memorizing.

Group of the following methods deal with data *transformation*:

- `toArray`: Converts an array of object data to an array with keys requested in
  the `$keys` array
- `toXml`: Converts object data into an XML string
- `toJson`: Converts object data to JSON
- `toString`: Converts object data into a string with a predefined format
- `serialize`: Converts object data into a string with defined keys and values

The other groups of these methods, implemented through the magic `__call` method,
enables the following neat syntax:

- `get<AttributeName>`, for example, `$object->getPackagingOption()`
- `set<AttributeName>`, for example,
  `$object->setPackagingOption('plastic_bag')`
- `uns<AttributeName>`, for example, `$object->unsPackagingOption()`
- `has<AttributeName>`, for example, `$object->hasPackagingOption()`

To quickly put this magic into perspective, let's manually create the
`magelicious_core_log` table as follows:

```
CREATE TABLE `magelicious_core_log` (
  `entity_id` int(10) unsigned NOT NULL AUTO_INCREMENT,
  `severity_level` varchar(24) NOT NULL,
  `note` text NOT NULL,
  `created_at` timestamp NOT NULL DEFAULT CURRENT_TIMESTAMP ON UPDATE
CURRENT_TIMESTAMP,
  PRIMARY KEY (`entity_id`)
) ENGINE=InnoDB DEFAULT CHARSET=utf8;
```

With the magic of `DataObject`, our empty `Magelicious\Core\Model\Log` model will still be able to save its data, as follows:

```
$log->setCreatedAt(new \DateTime());
$log->setSeverityLevel('info');
$log->setNote('Just Some Note');
$log->save();
```

While this example would work, there is far more to it than this. Creating tables manually is not a viable option for building modules. Magento has just the right mechanism for this, which is called *setup scripts*.

Working with setup scripts

Every time a module is installed via a `php bin/magento module:enable` command, Magento shows the following message: **To make sure that the enabled modules are properly registered, run 'setup:upgrade'**. The `php bin/magento setup:upgrade` command upgrades the Magento application, database data, and schema. Once triggered, the upgrade command instantiates `Magento\Setup\Model\Installer`, which then goes through a series of methods. Its `getSchemaDataHandler` method reveals the types of available *setup scripts*:

- `InstallSchema.php`
- `UpgradeSchema.php`
- `Recurring.php`
- `InstallData.php`
- `UpgradeData.php`
- `RecurringData.php`

These scripts live under the `<VendorName>/<ModuleName>/Setup` directory.

Once successfully finished, the `setup:upgrade` command makes a new entry, or updates an existing one, in the `setup_module` table. There, we can see the `schema_version` and `data_version` values logged against each `module`.

> When testing out setup scripts, we can manually delete and adjust our module entries under the `setup_module` table to trigger individual type of setup script. For example, we can leave `schema_version` as is, while changing the `data_version`.

Let's take a closer look at writing each of those scripts.

The InstallSchema script

The InstallSchema script is used when we wish to add new columns to existing tables or create new tables. This script is run only when a module is enabled. Once enabled, the module gets a corresponding entry under the setup_module.schema_version table column. This entry prevents the InstallSchema script running on any subsequent setup:upgrade command where the module's setup_version remains the same.

Let's go ahead and create the <MAGELICIOUS_DIR>/Core/Setup/InstallSchema.php file with the following content:

```
use \Magento\Framework\Setup\InstallSchemaInterface;
use Magento\Framework\Setup\ModuleContextInterface;
use Magento\Framework\Setup\SchemaSetupInterface;

class InstallSchema implements InstallSchemaInterface {
    public function install(SchemaSetupInterface $setup,
ModuleContextInterface $context) {
        $setup->startSetup();
        echo 'InstallSchema->install()' . PHP_EOL;
        $setup->endSetup();
    }
}
```

The use of $setup->startSetup(); and $setup->endSetup(); is a common practice among the majority of setup scripts. The implementation of these two methods deals with running additional environment setup steps, such as setting SQL_MODE and FOREIGN_KEY_CHECKS, as can be seen under Magento\Framework\DB\Adapter\Pdo\Mysql.

To make something useful out of it, let's go ahead and replace the echo line with the code that actually creates our magelicious_core_log table:

```
$table = $setup->getConnection()
    ->newTable($setup->getTable('magelicious_core_log'))
    ->addColumn(
        'entity_id',
        \Magento\Framework\DB\Ddl\Table::TYPE_INTEGER,
        null,
        ['identity' => true, 'unsigned' => true, 'nullable' => false,
'primary' => true],
        'Entity ID'
    )->addColumn(
        'severity_level',
```

```
        \Magento\Framework\DB\Ddl\Table::TYPE_TEXT,
        24,
        ['nullable' => false],
        'Severity Level'
    )->addColumn(
        'note',
        \Magento\Framework\DB\Ddl\Table::TYPE_TEXT,
        null,
        ['nullable' => false],
        'Note'
    )->addColumn(
        'created_at',
        \Magento\Framework\DB\Ddl\Table::TYPE_TIMESTAMP,
        null,
        ['nullable' => false],
        'Created At'
    )->setComment('Magelicious Core Log Table');
$setup->getConnection()->createTable($table);
```

`$setup->getConnection()` gets us the database adapter instance. From there on, we get access to methods that are needed for database table creation. When it comes to `InstallSchema` scripts, the majority of the time, the following methods will do the job:

- `newTable`: Retrieves a DDL object for the new table
- `addColumn`: Adds columns to the table
- `addIndex`: Adds an index to the table
- `addForeignKey`: Adds a foreign key to the table
- `setComment`: Sets a comment for the table
- `createTable`: Creates a table from a DDL object

The `magelicious_core_log` table here is essentially storage behind our `Magelicious\Core\Model\Log` *simple* model. If our model was an EAV model, we would be using the same `InstallSchema` script to create tables such as the following:

- `log_entity`
- `log_entity_datetime`
- `log_entity_decimal`
- `log_entity_int`
- `log_entity_text`
- `log_entity_varchar`

However, in the case of the EAV model, the actual attributes `severity_level` and `note` would then likely be added via an `InstallData` script. This is because attributes definitions are essentially data under the `eav_attribute_*` tables—primarily the `eav_attribute` table. Therefore, attributes are created inside of the `InstallData` and `UpgradeData` scripts.

The UpgradeSchema script

The `UpgradeSchema` script is used when we wish to create new tables or add columns to existing tables. Given that it is run on every `setup:upgrade`, where `setup_module.schema_version` is lower than `setup_version` under `<VendorName>/<ModuleName>/etc/module.xml`, we are in charge of controlling the code for a specific version. This is usually done via the *if-ed* `version_compare` approach.

To better demonstrate this, let's create the `<MAGELICIOUS_DIR>/Core/Setup/UpgradeSchema.php` file with the following content:

```
use \Magento\Framework\Setup\UpgradeSchemaInterface;
use Magento\Framework\Setup\ModuleContextInterface;
use Magento\Framework\Setup\SchemaSetupInterface;

class UpgradeSchema implements UpgradeSchemaInterface {
    public function upgrade(SchemaSetupInterface $setup,
ModuleContextInterface $context) {
        $setup->startSetup();
        if (version_compare($context->getVersion(), '2.0.2') < 0) {
            $this->upgradeToVersionTwoZeroTwo($setup);
        }
        $setup->endSetup();
    }

    private function upgradeToVersionTwoZeroTwo(SchemaSetupInterface
$setup) {
        echo 'UpgradeSchema->upgradeToVersionTwoZeroTwo()' . PHP_EOL;
    }
}
```

The *if-ed* `version_compare` here reads as follows: *if the current module version is equal to 2.0.2, then execute* the `upgradeToVersionTwoZeroTwo` *method*. If we were to release an updated version of our module, we would need to properly bump up the `setup_version` of `<VendorName>/<ModuleName>/etc/module.xml`, or else `UpgradeSchema` does not make a lot of sense. Likewise, we should always be sure to target a specific module version, thus avoiding code that executes on every version change.

When it comes to `UpgradeSchema` scripts, the following methods of a database adapter instance, alongside the previously mentioned one, will be of interest:

- `dropColumn`: Drops the column from a table
- `dropForeignKey`: Drops the foreign key from a table
- `dropIndex`: Drops the index from a table
- `dropTable`: Drops the table from a database
- `modifyColumn`: Modifies the column definition

The Recurring script

The `Recurring` scripts executes on each and every `setup:upgrade` command, regardless of the `schema_version` or `data_version` logged against the `setup_module` table.

Let's create the `<MAGELICIOUS_DIR>/Core/Setup/Recurring.php` file with the following content:

```
use Magento\Framework\Setup\InstallSchemaInterface;
use Magento\Framework\Setup\ModuleContextInterface;
use Magento\Framework\Setup\SchemaSetupInterface;

class Recurring implements InstallSchemaInterface {
    public function install(SchemaSetupInterface $setup,
ModuleContextInterface $context) {
        $setup->startSetup();
        echo 'Recurring->install()' . PHP_EOL;
        $setup->endSetup();
    }
}
```

Though interesting, the `Recurring` scripts are rarely used in Magento. Only a handful of them are used, and that is mostly for installing external foreign keys. This is not to say that we cannot use them for our purposes – it is just that their use case is quite limited when we think about it.

The InstallData script

The `InstallData` script is used when we wish to add new data to existing tables. This script is run only when a module is enabled. Once enabled, the module gets a corresponding entry under the `setup_module.data_version` table column. This entry prevents the `InstallData` script to run on any subsequent `setup:upgrade` command execution, where the module's `setup_version` remains the same.

Let's create the `<MAGELICIOUS_DIR>/Core/Setup/InstallData.php` file with the following content:

```
use \Magento\Framework\Setup\InstallDataInterface;
use Magento\Framework\Setup\ModuleContextInterface;
use Magento\Framework\Setup\ModuleDataSetupInterface;

class InstallData implements InstallDataInterface {
    public function install(ModuleDataSetupInterface $setup,
ModuleContextInterface $context) {
        $setup->startSetup();
        echo 'InstallData->install()' . PHP_EOL;
        $setup->endSetup();
    }
}
```

Chances are, we will be interacting with this type of script more often than not. Replacing the `echo` line with modified pieces of the equivalent Magento `InstallData` script might give us a better understanding of the possibilities behind these scripts.

The UpgradeData script

Let's create the `<MAGELICIOUS_DIR>/Core/Setup/UpgradeData.php` file with the following content:

```
use Magento\Framework\Setup\ModuleContextInterface;
use Magento\Framework\Setup\ModuleDataSetupInterface;

class UpgradeData implements \Magento\Framework\Setup\UpgradeDataInterface
{
    public function upgrade(ModuleDataSetupInterface $setup,
ModuleContextInterface $context) {
 $setup->startSetup();
 if (version_compare($context->getVersion(), '2.0.2') < 0) {
 $this->upgradeToVersionTwoZeroTwo($setup);
 }
```

```
$setup->endSetup();
    }

    private function upgradeToVersionTwoZeroTwo(ModuleDataSetupInterface
$setup) {
        echo 'UpgradeData->upgradeToVersionTwoZeroTwo()' . PHP_EOL;
    }
}
```

Let's go ahead and replace the echo line with something practical, like adding a new column to an existing table:

```
$salesSetup = $this->salesSetupFactory->create(['setup' => $setup]);
$salesSetup->addAttribute('order', 'merchant_note', [
    'type' => \Magento\Framework\DB\Ddl\Table::TYPE_TEXT,
    'visible' => false,
    'required' => false
]);
```

Here, we used the instance of Magento\Sales\Setup\SalesSetupFactory, injected through __construct. This further creates an instance of the Magento\Sales\Setup\SalesSetup class. We need this class in order to create sales EAV attributes. The *order* entity is somewhat of a strange mix; while it is registered as an EAV type of entity under the eav_entity_type table, it does not really use eav_attribute_* tables – it uses a single sales_order table to store its attributes. We could have easily used (Install|Upgrade)Schema scripts to simply add a new column via $setup->getConnection()->addColumn(). Once executed, this code adds the merchant_note column to the sales_order table. We will use this column later on, as we reach the *Extending entities* section.

The RecurringData script

Much like recurring scripts, the RecurringData scripts are rarely used in Magento. They also execute on each and every setup:upgrade command, regardless of the schema_version or data_version logged against the setup_module table. Magento Open Source uses merely three RecurringData scripts throughout its codebase.

Let's create the <MAGELICIOUS_DIR>/Core/Setup/RecurringData.php file with the following content:

```
use Magento\Framework\Setup\InstallDataInterface;
use Magento\Framework\Setup\ModuleContextInterface;
use Magento\Framework\Setup\ModuleDataSetupInterface;
```

```
class RecurringData implements InstallDataInterface {
    public function install(ModuleDataSetupInterface $setup,
ModuleContextInterface $context) {
        $setup->startSetup();
        echo 'RecurringData->install()' . PHP_EOL;
        $setup->endSetup();
    }
}
```

The setup scripts provide a way for us to manage the data and its representation in the database. Whereas adding a new attribute to *simple model* is likely a case of extending its table by an extra column (*Schema scripts), adding a new attribute to an *EAV model* is a matter of adding new data under the eav_attribute table (*Data scripts).

Extending entities

We extend entities by adding additional attributes to them. Referring back to the magical *getter* and *setter* methods mentioned in the context of Magento\Framework\DataObject, the logical thinking might be: *what's the big deal; can't we just add new database columns via* UpgradeSchema *and use magical getter and setter methods to go around it?* The answer is both *yes* and *no*, but mainly leaning toward *no* – we will soon learn why.

To better explain this, let's take a look at Magento\Sales\Model\Order, the entity model. This model implements the Magento\Sales\Api\Data\OrderInterface interface, which further extends Magento\Framework\Api\ExtensibleDataInterface. Here, we can see a constant defining a key for the extension attributes object. This is somewhat of a starting point for extending entities. Suffice to say, there is an extra abstraction layer on top of some of the models. This abstraction layer, called *service contracts*, is a set of PHP interfaces that ensure a well-defined, durable API that other modules and third-party extensions might implement.

This, however, is easier said than done. When you think about it, if we had a module that's already heavily in use, adding even a simple attribute to one of its entity models might break its functionality. This is where extension attributes come into the picture.

Creating extension attributes

Creating a new *extension attribute* for an existing entity is usually a case of doing the following:

1. Using *setup scripts* to set the attribute, column, or table for persistence
2. Defining the extension attribute via `<VendorName>/<ModuleName>/etc/extension_attributes.xml`
3. Adding an *after and/or before* plugin to the `save`, `get`, and `getList` methods of an entity *repository*

Moving forward, we are going to create extension attributes for the *order* entity, that is, `customer_note` and `merchant_note`.

We can imagine `customer_note` as an attribute that does not persist its value(s) in the `sales_order` table as order entity does, whereas `merchant_note` attribute does. This is why we created the `sales_order.merchant_note` column earlier via the `UpgradeData`

script.

Let's go ahead and create the `<MAGELICIOUS_DIR>/Core/Api/Data/CustomerNoteInterface.php` file with the following content:

```
interface CustomerNoteInterface extends
\Magento\Framework\Api\ExtensibleDataInterface
{
    const CREATED_BY = 'created_by';
    const NOTE = 'note';

    public function setCreatedBy($createdBy);
    public function getCreatedBy();
    public function setNote($note);
    public function getNote();
}
```

The `customer_note` attribute is going to be a full-blown object, so we will create an interface for it.

While omitted in the example, be sure to set the *doc blocks* on each method, otherwise the Magento web API will throw an **Each getter must have a doc block** error once we hook up the plugin methods.

We will then create the `<MAGELICIOUS_DIR>/Core/Model/CustomerNote.php` file with the following content:

```
class CustomerNote extends \Magento\Framework\Model\AbstractExtensibleModel
implements \Magelicious\Core\Api\Data\CustomerNoteInterface
{
    public function setCreatedBy($createdBy) {
        return $this->setData(self::CREATED_BY, $createdBy);
    }

    public function getCreatedBy() {
        return $this->getData(self::CREATED_BY);
    }

    public function getNote() {
        return $this->getData(self::NOTE);
    }

    public function setNote($note) {
        return $this->setData(self::NOTE, $note);
    }
}
```

This class is essentially our `customer_note` entity model. To keep things minimal, we will just implement the `CustomerNoteInterface`, without any extra logic.

We will then go ahead and create the `<MAGELICIOUS_DIR>/Core/etc/extension_attributes.xml` file with the following content:

```
<?xml version="1.0"?>

<config>
    <extension_attributes for="Magento\Sales\Api\Data\OrderInterface">
        <attribute code="customer_note"
type="Magelicious\Core\Api\Data\CustomerNoteInterface"/>
        <attribute code="merchant_note" type="string"/>
    </extension_attributes>
</config>
```

The `extension_attributes.xml` file is where we register our extension attributes. The `type` argument allows us to register either complex types, such as an interface, or scalar types, such as a string or integer. With the extension attributes registered, it is time to register the corresponding plugins. This is done via the `di.xml` file.

Let's go ahead and create the `<MAGELICIOUS_DIR>/Core/etc/di.xml` file with the following content:

```xml
<?xml version="1.0"?>

<config>
    <preference for="Magelicious\Core\Api\Data\CustomerNoteInterface"
type="Magelicious\Core\Model\CustomerNote"/>
    <type name="Magento\Sales\Api\OrderRepositoryInterface">
        <plugin name="customerNoteToOrderRepository"
type="Magelicious\Core\Plugin\CustomerNoteToOrderRepository"/>
        <plugin name="merchantNoteToOrderRepository"
type="Magelicious\Core\Plugin\MerchantNoteToOrderRepository"/>
    </type>
</config>
```

The reason for registering plugins in the first place is to have our `customer_note` and `merchant_note` attributes available on the `getList`, `get`, and `save` methods of the `Magento\Sales\Api\OrderRepositoryInterface` interface. The repository interfaces are the main way of *CRUD-ing* entities under service contracts. Without proper plugins, Magento simply would not see our attributes.

Let's create the `<MAGELICIOUS_DIR>/Core/Plugin/CustomerNoteToOrderRepository.php` file with the following content:

```php
class CustomerNoteToOrderRepository {
    protected $orderExtensionFactory;
    protected $customerNoteInterfaceFactory;

    public function __construct(
        \Magento\Sales\Api\Data\OrderExtensionFactory
$orderExtensionFactory,
        \Magelicious\Core\Api\Data\CustomerNoteInterfaceFactory
$customerNoteInterfaceFactory
    ) {
        $this->orderExtensionFactory = $orderExtensionFactory;
        $this->customerNoteInterfaceFactory =
$customerNoteInterfaceFactory;
    }
```

```
        private function getCustomerNoteAttribute(
            \Magento\Sales\Api\Data\OrderInterface $resultOrder
        ) {
            $extensionAttributes = $resultOrder->getExtensionAttributes() ?:
$this->orderExtensionFactory->create();

            // TODO: Get customer note from somewhere (below we fake it)
            $customerNote = $this->customerNoteInterfaceFactory->create()
                ->setCreatedBy('Mark')
                ->setNote('The note ' . \time());

            $extensionAttributes->setCustomerNote($customerNote);
            $resultOrder->setExtensionAttributes($extensionAttributes);
            return $resultOrder;
        }

        private function saveCustomerNoteAttribute(
            \Magento\Sales\Api\Data\OrderInterface $resultOrder
        ) {
            $extensionAttributes = $resultOrder->getExtensionAttributes();
            if ($extensionAttributes &&
$extensionAttributes->getCustomerNote()) {
                // TODO: Save $extensionAttributes->getCustomerNote() somewhere
            }
            return $resultOrder;
        }
    }
```

Right now, there are no plugin methods defined. `getCustomerNoteAttribute`
and `saveCustomerNoteAttribute` are essentially *helper* methods that we will soon use.

Let's extend our `CustomerNoteToOrderRepository` class by adding the `after` plugin for
the `getList` method, as follows:

```
public function afterGetList(
    \Magento\Sales\Api\OrderRepositoryInterface $subject,
    \Magento\Sales\Model\ResourceModel\Order\Collection $resultOrder
) {
    foreach ($resultOrder->getItems() as $order) {
        $this->afterGet($subject, $order);
    }
    return $resultOrder;
}
```

Now, let's extend our `CustomerNoteToOrderRepository` class by adding the `after` plugin for the `get` method, as follows:

```
public function afterGet(
    \Magento\Sales\Api\OrderRepositoryInterface $subject,
    \Magento\Sales\Api\Data\OrderInterface $resultOrder
) {
    $resultOrder = $this->getCustomerNoteAttribute($resultOrder);
    return $resultOrder;
}
```

Finally, let's extend our `CustomerNoteToOrderRepository` class by adding the `after` plugin for the `save` method, as follows:

```
public function afterSave(
    \Magento\Sales\Api\OrderRepositoryInterface $subject,
    \Magento\Sales\Api\Data\OrderInterface $resultOrder
) {
    $resultOrder = $this->saveCustomerNoteAttribute($resultOrder);
    return $resultOrder;
}
```

With the plugins for `customer_note` sorted, let's go ahead and address the plugins for `merchant_note`. We will create the `<MAGELICIOUS_DIR>/Core/Plugin/MerchantNoteToOrderRepository.php` file with the following content:

```
class MerchantNoteToOrderRepository {
    protected $orderExtensionFactory;

    public function __construct(
        \Magento\Sales\Api\Data\OrderExtensionFactory
$orderExtensionFactory
    ) {
        $this->orderExtensionFactory = $orderExtensionFactory;
    }

    private function getMerchantNoteAttribute(
        \Magento\Sales\Api\Data\OrderInterface $order
    ) {
        $extensionAttributes = $order->getExtensionAttributes() ?:
$this->orderExtensionFactory->create();
$extensionAttributes->setMerchantNote($order->getData('merchant_note'));
        $order->setExtensionAttributes($extensionAttributes);
        return $order;
    }
```

```
        private function saveMerchantNoteAttribute(
            \Magento\Sales\Api\Data\OrderInterface $order
        ) {
            $extensionAttributes = $order->getExtensionAttributes();
            if ($extensionAttributes &&
    $extensionAttributes->getMerchantNote()) {
                $order->setData('merchant_note',
    $extensionAttributes->getMerchantNote());
            }
            return $order;
        }
    }
```

Right now, there are no plugin methods defined. getMerchantNoteAttribute and saveMerchantNoteAttribute are essentially helper methods that we will soon use.

Let's extend our MerchantNoteToOrderRepository class by adding the *after* plugin for the getList method, as follows:

```
public function afterGetList(
    \Magento\Sales\Api\OrderRepositoryInterface $subject,
    \Magento\Sales\Model\ResourceModel\Order\Collection $order
) {
    foreach ($order->getItems() as $_order) {
        $this->afterGet($subject, $_order);
    }
    return $order;
}
```

Now, let's extend our MerchantNoteToOrderRepository class by adding the after plugin for the get method, as follows:

```
public function afterGet(
    \Magento\Sales\Api\OrderRepositoryInterface $subject,
    \Magento\Sales\Api\Data\OrderInterface $order
) {
    $order = $this->getMerchantNoteAttribute($order);
    return $order;
}
```

Finally, let's extend our `MerchantNoteToOrderRepository` class by adding the `before` plugin for the `save` method, as follows:

```
public function beforeSave (
    \Magento\Sales\Api\OrderRepositoryInterface $subject,
    \Magento\Sales\Api\Data\OrderInterface $order
) {
    $order = $this->saveMerchantNoteAttribute($order);
    return [$order];
}
```

The obvious difference here is that, with `MerchantNoteToOrderRepository`, we are using `beforeSave`, whereas we used `afterSave` with `CustomerNoteToOrderRepository`. The reason for this is that `merchant_note` is to be saved directly on the entity whose repository we are plugging into, that is, its table in the `sales_order` database. This way, we use its `Magento\Framework\DataObject` properties of `setData` to fetch what was assumingly note already set via extension attributes and pass it onto the object's `merchant_note` property before it is saved. Magento's built-in save mechanism then takes over and stores the property, as long as the corresponding column exists in the database.

With the plugins in place, our attributes should now be visible and persistable when used through the `OrderRepositoryInterface`. Without getting too deep into the web API at this point, we can quickly test this via performing the following REST request:

```
GET
/index.php/rest/V1/orders?searchCriteria[filter_groups][0][filters][0][fiel
d]=entity_id&searchCriteria[filter_groups][0][filters][0][value]=1
Host: magelicious.loc
Content-Type: application/json
Authorization: Bearer 0vq6d4kabpxgc5kysb2sybf3n4ct771x
```

Whereas the `Bearer` token is something we get by running the following REST login action:

```
POST /index.php/rest/V1/integration/admin/token
Host: magelicious.loc
Content-Type: application/json
{"username": "john", "password": "grdM%0i9a49n"}
```

The successful response of GET /V1/orders should yield a result of the following partial structure:

```
{
  "items": [
    {
      "extension_attributes": {
        "shipping_assignments": [...],
        "customer_note": {
          "created_by": "Mark",
          "note": "Note ABC"
        },
        "merchant_note": "Note XYZ"
      }
    }
  ]
}
```

We can see that our two attributes are nicely nested within the extension_attributes key.

> Postman, the API development tool, makes it easy to test APIs.
> See https://www.getpostman.com for more information.

The OrderRepositoryInterface to web API REST relationship maps out as follows:

- getList: GET /V1/orders (*plus the search criteria part*)
- get: GET /V1/orders/:id
- save: POST /V1/orders/create

We will learn more about the web API in the next chapter. The example given here was merely for the purpose of visualizing the work we have done around plugins. Using extension attributes, with the help of plugins, we have essentially extended the Magento web API.

Summary

Throughout this chapter, we learned how to differentiate the three types of Magento models: *non-persistable*, *persistable simple*, and *persistable EAV*. The inners of EAV models are left out of scope due to their inherently complex nature. We then took a look through six different setup scripts. These give us a great deal of flexibility over schema and data management. Combined with extension attributes, we get a powerful mechanism for extending built-in entities. Though somewhat tedious, the extension attributes mechanism use of interfaces ensures that integrators can extend this built-in functionality with complex data types.

Moving forward, we are going to take a look at the powerful web API that's implemented in Magento.

3
Understanding Web APIs

Web **application programming interfaces** (**API**) play a major role in modern application development. They allow various third-party integrators to interact with applications through the HTTP layer. Magento supports both **Representational State Transfer** (**REST**) and **Simple Object Access Protocol** (**SOAP**) APIs. Its web API framework is based on the **create, read, update, delete** (**CRUD**) and **search** (*search criteria*) models. The scope of functionality that APIs offer is quite big, allowing us to use them for a wide range of tasks, such as creating a completely new shopping application, integrating with **customer relationship management** (**CRM**) systems, **enterprise resource planning** (**ERP**) systems, and **content management systems** (**CMS**), as well as creating JavaScript widgets in the Magento storefront itself.

Moving forward, we are going to take a closer look at the following web API sections:

- Types of users
- Types of authentication
- Types of endpoints
- Using existing Web APIs
- Creating custom Web APIs
- Understanding search criteria

Technical requirements

You will need to have basic knowledge of PHP, OOP, JavaScript, and XML. You will also need Apache, MySQL, and AMPPS installed on your system to execute the codes.

The code files of this chapter can be found on GitHub:
`https://github.com/PacktPublishing/Magento-2-Quick-Start-Guide.`

Check out the following video to see the Code in Action:

`http://bit.ly/2Oz3Gqs.`

Types of users

The Magento web API framework differentiates three fundamental types of users:

- **Guest**: Authorized against an `anonymous` resource:

```
<resources>
  <resource ref="anonymous" />
</resources>
```

- **Customer**: Authorized against a `self` resource:

```
<resources>
  <resource ref="self"/>
</resources>
```

- **Integrator**: Authorized against a specific *resource* defined in `acl.xml`:

```
<resources>
  <resource ref="Magento_Cms::save"" />
</resources>
```

To further understand what this means, we need to understand the link between `<VendorName>/<ModuleName>/acl.xml` and `<VendorName>/<ModuleName>/webapi.xml`.

The `acl.xml` is where we define our access resources. Let's take a closer look at the partial extract of one such resource, defined in the `<MAGENTO_DIR>/module-cms/etc/acl.xml` file:

```
<config>
  <acl>
    <resources>
      <resource id="Magento_Backend::admin">
        <resource id="Magento_Backend::content">
          <resource id="Magento_Backend::content_elements">
            <resource id="Magento_Cms::page" title="Pages">
              <resource id="Magento_Cms::save" title="Save Page"/>
            </resource>
          </resource>
        </resource>
      </resource>
    </resources>
  </acl>
</config>
```

Our focus here is on the `Magento_Cms::save` resource. Magento merges all of these individual `acl.xml` files into one big *ACL tree*. We can see this tree in two places in the Magento admin area:

- The **Role Resource** tab of the **System | Permissions | User Roles | Edit | Add New Role** screen
- The **API** tab of the **System | Extensions | Integrations | Edit | Add New Integration** screen:

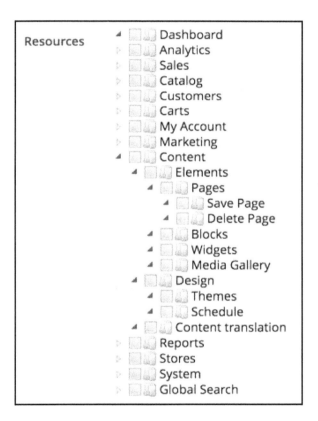

These are the two screens where we define access permissions for a *standard admin user* and a special *web API integrator user*. This is not to say that a standard admin user cannot execute web API calls. The difference will become more obvious when we get to the *Types of authentication* section.

To this point, these resources don't really do anything on their own. Simply defining them within `acl.xml` won't magically make a CMS page in this case access-protected, or anything like that. This is where controllers come into the mix, as one example of an access-controlling mechanism. A quick lookup against `Magento_Cms::save` string usage, reveals a `Magento\Cms\Controller\Adminhtml\Page\Edit` class using it as part of its `const ADMIN_RESOURCE = 'Magento_Cms::save'` definition.

The `ADMIN_RESOURCE` constant is defined further down the inheritance chain, on the `\Magento\Backend\App\AbstractAction` as `const ADMIN_RESOURCE = 'Magento_Backend::admin'`. This is further used by the `_isAllowed` method implementation as follows:

```
protected function _isAllowed()
{
  return $this->_authorization->isAllowed(static::ADMIN_RESOURCE);
}
```

The `AbstractAction` class here is the basis for pretty much any Magento admin controller. This means that the controller is the one that utilizes the resource defined in `acl.xml`, whereas definitions in `acl.xml` serve the purpose of building the ACL tree, which we can manage from the Magento admin interface. This means that anyone trying to access the `cms/page/edit` URL in admin must have a `Magento_Cms::save` resource permission to do so. Otherwise, the `_isAllowed` method, reading the `ADMIN_RESOURCE` value, will return `false` and forbid access to the page.

Web APIs, on the other hand, don't use controllers, so there is no access to the `ADMIN_RESOURCE` constant and the `_isAllowed` method. APIs use `webapi.xml` to define `routes`. Let's follow up with the *CMS page save* analogue, as per the `<MAGENTO_DIR>/module-cms/etc/webapi.xml` file:

```
<routes>
  <route url="/V1/cmsPage" method="POST">
    <service class="Magento\Cms\Api\PageRepositoryInterface"
method="save"/>
    <resources>
      <resource ref="Magento_Cms::page"/>
    </resources>
  </route>
  <route url="/V1/cmsPage/:id" method="PUT">
    <service class="Magento\Cms\Api\PageRepositoryInterface"
method="save"/>
    <resources>
      <resource ref="Magento_Cms::page"/>
    </resources>
```

```
    </route>
  </routes>
```

The individual `route` definition binds together a few things. The `url` and `method` argument of a `route` element specify what URL will trigger this `route`. The `class` and `method` arguments of a `service` element specify which interface and method on that interface will execute once the route is triggered. Finally, the `ref` argument of a `resource` element specifies the security check to be executed. If a user executing a web API call is unauthenticated or authenticated with a role that does not have `Magento_Cms::page`, the request won't execute the service method specified.

The *customer* type of user is the most convenient for working with widgets. The Magento checkout is an excellent example of that. The whole checkout is a fully AJAX-enabled app on its own, separate from the *usual* Magento storefront, such as its CMS, category, and product pages.

Types of authentication

Magento supports three different types of authentication methods:

- **Session-based authentication**: Best suited for JavaScript widget applications running as part of the Magento storefront itself. Magento uses the *logged-in* state of an admin user or customer to verify their identity and authorize access to the requested resource.
- **Token-based authentication**: Best suited for mobile or other types of applications that wish to avoid the complexities of full-blown OAuth-based authentication. To obtain the token (*with REST*), one initially uses the `POST /V1/integration/customer/token` or the `POST /V1/integration/admin/token`. A successful response returns a random 32-character-long string, for example, `8pcvbwrp9715m1pvcdnis6e3930n4rsj`. This is our token, used for any subsequent API calls, via a header given as `Authorization: Bearer <token>`. The simplicity behind this authentication makes it an appealing choice for developers.

- **OAuth-based authentication**: Best suited for third-party applications that integrate with Magento on behalf of the user, without revealing or storing any user IDs or passwords. The starting point for setting up OAuth-based authentication is for a Magento admin user to create integration, under the **System | Extensions | Integration | Add New Integration** screen. Here we can provide options such as **Callback URL** and **Identity link URL**, which define the external application endpoint that receives the OAuth credentials. If given, the values of these links point to the external app that stands as the OAuth client. Successfully saved integration generates the key OAuth artefacts, such as *Consumer Key*, *Consumer Secret*, *Access Token*, and *Access Token Secret*.

Using OAuth-based authentication exceeds the scope of this book, which is why moving forward, all of our examples will use simpler *token-based authentication*.

Types of APIs

Magento supports two types of APIs:

- **Representational State Transfer** (**REST**): The endpoints for APIs depend on `webapi.xml` and the individual `url` arguments of each `route` element, as we will soon see. The authentication is carried over in a request's header via a *Bearer* token.
- **Simple Object Access Protocol** (**SOAP**) : The **Web Services Description Language (WSDL)** is available via a URL such as `http://magelicious.loc/soap/default?wsdlservices=catalogProductRepositoryV1`. Whereas the `default` string is optional, and it matches the code name of the Magento store in this case, if omitted, Magento will default to a default store, whatever its code might be. Likewise, the `services` parameter accepts one or more (*comma-separated*) lists of services. The full list of available services can be obtained via a URL such as `http://magelicious.loc/soap/default?wsdl_list`. Without going into the details of it, suffice it to say that Magento generates the service names automatically based on module and interface names. Much like with REST APIs, the authentication is carried over in a request's header via a *Bearer* token.

The great thing about these two is that we don't get to write two different APIs in Magento. The approach to writing APIs is unified, so to speak. We define some interfaces, classes, and configurations, and Magento then generates the API endpoints for both REST and SOAP on its own. Thus, the *REST vs. SOAP* choice really only becomes a question when we consume APIs, not while we write them.

Using SOAP services exceeds the scope of this book, which is why moving forward, all of our examples will use *REST* APIs.

Using existing web APIs

The *CRUD* and *search* models of web APIs are implemented through a set of `*RepositoryInterface` interfaces, found in the `<VendorName>/<ModuleName>/Api/<EntityName>RepositoryInterface.php` files.

The majority of these *repository interfaces* define a specific set of common methods:

- save
- get
- getById
- getList
- delete
- deleteById

The data type that *flows* through these methods follows a certain pattern, where each entity passing through an API has a data interface defined in a `<VendorName>/<ModuleName>/Api/Data/<EntityName>Interface.php` file.

Let's take a closer look at `<MAGENTO_DIR>/module-cms/Api/BlockRepositoryInterface.php`:

```
interface BlockRepositoryInterface
{
    public function save(
        \Magento\Cms\Api\Data\BlockInterface $block
    );
    public function getById($blockId);
    public function getList(
        \Magento\Framework\Api\SearchCriteriaInterface $searchCriteria
    );
    public function delete(
        \Magento\Cms\Api\Data\BlockInterface $block
    );
    public function deleteById($blockId);
}
```

The concrete implementations of *repository* interfaces can usually be found in the `<VendorName>/<ModuleName>/Model/<EntityName>Repository.php` or the `<VendorName>/<ModuleName>/Model/ResourceModel/<EntityName>Repository.php` files. The exact location is not that relevant, as `webapi.xml` should always use an *interface* for a `class` argument for its `service` element definition. The mapping between the *interface* and *concrete* implementation then happens in the module's `di.xml` file via a `preference` definition. From an integrator's point of view, using APIs does not require any knowledge of concrete implementations.

 The PHPDoc `@return` tag is a requirement for every getter method on an API interface, otherwise, **Each getter must have a doc block** error is thrown.

The **Swagger** URL, `http://magelicious.loc/swagger`, will generate a Swagger UI interface, that allows us to visualize and interact with the API's resources:

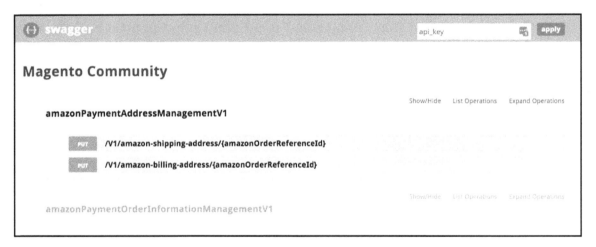

By default, documentation returned here is limited to *anonymous* users only. Generating a valid API key, via the `POST /V1/integration/customer/token` or `POST /V1/integration/admin/token` will unlock the documentation for all the resources available to a given user. While Swagger certainly has its place in development workflows, oftentimes the Postman tool is a more robust solution for those working extensively with APIs.

Let's go ahead and *CRUD* our way through the `cmsBlock` interface, using REST endpoints:

- `save` (create a new block) `POST /V1/cmsBlock`
- `save` (update an existing block by `id`) `PUT /V1/cmsBlock/:id`
- `getById` (get an existing block by `id`) `GET /V1/cmsBlock/:blockId`
- `deleteById` (delete an existing block) `DELETE /V1/cmsBlock/:blockId`
- `getList` (get an array of existing blocks) `GET /V1/cmsBlock/search`

We will be using the *integrator* type of user. This will be our Magento admin user, assigned either full resources, or at least the **Resources | Content | Elements | Blocks** resource under the **Role Resource** tab of the **System | Permissions | User Roles | Edit | Add New Role** screen.

We start with the admin login request, in order to obtain a *token* for later requests:

```
POST /index.php/rest/V1/integration/admin/token HTTP/1.1
Host: magelicious.loc
Content-Type: application/json
{
  "username": "branko",
  "password": "jrdJ%0i9a69n"
}
```

The successful JSON response should contain our API token, which we will be using for any subsequent API calls. The token itself is stored in the `oauth_token` table, under the `token` column. We further have `consumer_id`, `admin_id`, and `customer_id` columns in that table. These get filled depending on the user type we used to log in. Both `consumer_id` and `admin_id` are of the *integrator* type. These columns get filled accordingly depending on the user and authentication types used; as in *customer* versus *integrator*, and *token-based* vs *OAuth-based* vs *session-based* authentication.

Now let's create a new block via `POST /V1/cmsBlock`; this triggers the `save` method:

```
POST /rest/V1/cmsBlock HTTP/1.1
Host: magelicious.loc
Content-Type: application/json
Authorization: Bearer 8pcvbwrp9715m1pvcdnis6e3930n4rsj
{
  "block": {
    "identifier": "x-block",
    "title": "The X Block",
    "content": "<p>The <strong>X Block</strong> Content...</p>",
    "active": true
  }
}
```

The successful JSON response should return our newly created block:

```
{
    "id": 1,
    "identifier": "x-block",
    "title": "The X Block",
    "content": "<p>The <strong>X Block</strong> Content...</p>",
    "active": true
}
```

Now let's update the existing `cmsBlock` via `PUT /V1/cmsBlock/:id`; this triggers the `save` method:

```
PUT /rest/V1/cmsBlock/1 HTTP/1.1
Host: magelicious.loc
Content-Type: application/json
Authorization: Bearer 8pcvbwrp9715m1pvcdnis6e3930n4rsj
{
  "block": {
    "identifier": "y-block",
    "title": "The Y Block",
    "content": "<p>The <strong>Y Block</strong> Content...</p>",
    "active": true
  }
}
```

The successful JSON response should return the updated block:

```
{
    "id": 1,
    "identifier": "y-block",
    "title": "The Y Block",
    "content": "<p>The <strong>Y Block</strong> Content...</p>",
    "active": true
}
```

Let's now fetch one of the existing blocks via `GET /V1/cmsBlock/:blockId`; this triggers the `getById` method:

```
GET /rest/V1/cmsBlock/1 HTTP/1.1
Host: magelicious.loc
Content-Type: application/json
Authorization: Bearer 8pcvbwrp9715m1pvcdnis6e3930n4rsj
```

The successful JSON response is structurally identical to that of the `save` method.

Now, let's try deleting one of the blocks via `DELETE /V1/cmsBlock/:blockId`; this triggers the `deleteById` method:

```
DELETE /rest/V1/cmsBlock/2 HTTP/1.1
Host: magelicious.loc
Content-Type: application/json
Authorization: Bearer 8pcvbwrp9715m1pvcdnis6e3930n4rsj
```

The successful JSON response returns a single `true` or `false`.

Finally, let's try fetching the list of blocks via `GET /V1/cmsBlock/search`; this triggers the `getList` method:

```
GET
/rest/V1/cmsBlock/search?searchCriteria[filter_groups][0][filters][0][field
]=title&amp;searchCriteria[filter_groups][0][filters][0][value]=%Block%&amp
;searchCriteria[filter_groups][0][filters][0][condition_type]=like HTTP/1.1
Host: magelicious.loc
Content-Type: application/json
Authorization: Bearer 8pcvbwrp9715m1pvcdnis6e3930n4rsj
```

Sadly, the GET request does not allow for the body, so `?searchCriteria...` has to be passed via a URL.

The successful JSON response returns an object comprised of `items`, `search_criteria`, and `total_count` top-level keys:

```json
{
    "items": [
        {
            "id": 4,
            "identifier": "x-block",
            "title": "The X Block",
            "content": "The <strong>X Block</strong> Content...",
            "creation_time": "2018-06-23 07:30:06",
            "update_time": "2018-06-23 07:30:06",
            "active": true
        },
        {
            "id": 5,
            "identifier": "y-block",
            "title": "The Y Block",
            "content": "The <strong>Y Block</strong> Content...",
            "creation_time": "2018-06-23 07:30:14",
            "update_time": "2018-06-23 07:30:14",
            "active": true
        }
```

```
    ],
    "search_criteria": {...},
    "total_count": 2
}
```

We will address the `search_criteria` in more detail later on.

Creating custom web APIs

Let's go ahead and create a miniature, yet full-blown Magento module `Magelicious_Boxy` that demonstrates the entire flow of creating a custom web API.

We start off by defining a module `<MAGELICIOUS_DIR>/Boxy/registration.php` as follows:

```
\Magento\Framework\Component\ComponentRegistrar::register(
    \Magento\Framework\Component\ComponentRegistrar::MODULE,
    'Magelicious_Boxy',
    __DIR__
);
```

We then define the `<MAGELICIOUS_DIR>/Boxy/etc/module.xml` as follows:

```
<config>
    <module name="Magelicious_Boxy" setup_version="2.0.2"/>
</config>
```

We then define the `<MAGELICIOUS_DIR>/Boxy/Setup/InstallSchema.php` that adds the following table:

```
$table = $setup->getConnection()
  ->newTable($setup->getTable('magelicious_boxy_box'))
  ->addColumn(
    'entity_id',
    \Magento\Framework\DB\Ddl\Table::TYPE_INTEGER,
    null, [
    'identity' => true,
    'unsigned' => true,
    'nullable' => false,
    'primary' => true
  ], 'Entity ID'
  )
  ->addColumn(
    'title',
    \Magento\Framework\DB\Ddl\Table::TYPE_TEXT,
    32,
```

```
    ['nullable' => false], 'Title'
  )
  ->addColumn(
    'content',
    \Magento\Framework\DB\Ddl\Table::TYPE_TEXT,
    null,
    ['nullable' => false], 'Content'
  )
  ->setComment('Magelicious Boxy Box Table');
$setup->getConnection()->createTable($table);
```

We then define `<MAGELICIOUS_DIR>/Boxy/Api/Data/BoxInterface.php` as follows:

```
interface BoxInterface {
  const BOX_ID = 'box_id';
  const TITLE = 'title';
  const CONTENT = 'content';
  public function getId();
  public function getTitle();
  public function getContent();
  public function setId($id);
  public function setTitle($title);
  public function setContent($content);
}
```

We then define
`<MAGELICIOUS_DIR>/Boxy/Api/Data/BoxSearchResultsInterface.php` as follows:

```
interface BoxSearchResultsInterface extends
\Magento\Framework\Api\SearchResultsInterface
{
  public function getItems();
  public function setItems(array $items);
}
```

We then add the `<MAGELICIOUS_DIR>/Boxy/Api/BoxRepositoryInterface.php` as follows:

```
interface BoxRepositoryInterface
{
  public function save(\Magelicious\Boxy\Api\Data\BoxInterface $box);
  public function getById($boxId);
  public function getList(\Magento\Framework\Api\SearchCriteriaInterface
$searchCriteria);
  public function delete(\Magelicious\Boxy\Api\Data\BoxInterface $box);
  public function deleteById($boxId);
}
```

We then define the <MAGELICIOUS_DIR>/Boxy/Model/Box.php as follows:

```php
class Box extends \Magento\Framework\Model\AbstractModel implements
\Magelicious\Boxy\Api\Data\BoxInterface
{
  protected function _construct() {
    $this->_init(\Magelicious\Boxy\Model\ResourceModel\Box::class);
  }

  public function getId() {
    return $this->getData(self::BOX_ID);
  }

  public function getTitle() {
  return $this->getData(self::TITLE);
  }

  public function getContent() {
    return $this->getData(self::CONTENT);
  }

  public function setId($id) {
    return $this->setData(self::BOX_ID, $id);
  }

  public function setTitle($title) {
    return $this->setData(self::TITLE, $title);
  }

  public function setContent($content) {
    return $this->setData(self::CONTENT, $content);
  }
}
```

We then define the <MAGELICIOUS_DIR>/Boxy/Model/ResourceModel/Box.php as follows:

```php
class Box extends \Magento\Framework\Model\ResourceModel\Db\AbstractDb
{
  protected function _construct() {
    $this->_init('magelicious_boxy_box', 'entity_id');
  }
}
```

We then define the
`<MAGELICIOUS_DIR>/Boxy/Model/ResourceModel/Box/Collection.php` as follows:

```
class Collection
{
  protected function _construct() {
    $this->_init(
        \Magelicious\Boxy\Model\Box::class,
        \Magelicious\Boxy\Model\ResourceModel\Box::class
    );
  }
}
```

We then define the `<MAGELICIOUS_DIR>/Boxy/Model/BoxRepository.php` as follows:

```
class BoxRepository implements \Magelicious\Boxy\Api\BoxRepositoryInterface
{
  protected $boxFactory;
  protected $boxResourceModel;
  protected $searchResultsFactory;
  protected $collectionProcessor;

  public function __construct(
    \Magelicious\Boxy\Api\Data\BoxInterfaceFactory $boxFactory,
    \Magelicious\Boxy\Model\ResourceModel\Box $boxResourceModel,
    \Magelicious\Boxy\Api\Data\BoxSearchResultsInterfaceFactory
$searchResultsFactory,
    \Magento\Framework\Api\SearchCriteria\CollectionProcessorInterface
$collectionProcessor
  )
  {
    $this->boxFactory = $boxFactory;
    $this->boxResourceModel = $boxResourceModel;
    $this->searchResultsFactory = $searchResultsFactory;
    $this->collectionProcessor = $collectionProcessor;
  }
  // Todo...
}
```

Let's go ahead and amend the BoxRepository with the save method as follows:

```
public function save(\Magelicious\Boxy\Api\Data\BoxInterface $box)
{
  try {
    $this->boxResourceModel->save($box);
  } catch (\Exception $e) {
    throw new
\Magento\Framework\Exception\CouldNotSaveException(__($e->getMessage()));
  }
  return $box;
}
```

Let's go ahead and amend the BoxRepository with the getById method as follows:

```
public function getById($boxId) {
  $box = $this->boxFactory->create();
  $this->boxResourceModel->load($box, $boxId);
  if (!$box->getId()) {
    throw new \Magento\Framework\Exception\NoSuchEntityException(__('Box
with id "%1" does not exist.', $boxId));
  }
  return $box;
}
```

Let's go ahead and amend the BoxRepository with the getList method as follows:

```
public function getList(\Magento\Framework\Api\SearchCriteriaInterface
$searchCriteria) {
  $collection = $this->boxCollectionFactory->create();
  $this->collectionProcessor->process($searchCriteria, $collection);
  $searchResults = $this->searchResultsFactory->create();
  $searchResults->setSearchCriteria($searchCriteria);
  $searchResults->setItems($collection->getItems());
  $searchResults->setTotalCount($collection->getSize());
  return $searchResults;
}
```

Let's go ahead and amend the `BoxRepository` with the `delete` method as follows:

```
public function delete(\Magelicious\Boxy\Api\Data\BoxInterface $box) {
    try {
        $this->boxResourceModel->delete($box);
    } catch (\Exception $e) {
        throw new
\Magento\Framework\Exception\CouldNotDeleteException(__($e->getMessage()));
    }
    return true;
}
```

Let's go ahead and amend the `BoxRepository` with the `deleteById` method as follows:

```
public function deleteById($boxId) {
    return $this->delete($this->getById($boxId));
}
```

We then define the `<MAGELICIOUS_DIR>/Boxy/etc/di.xml` as follows:

```
<config>
    <preference for="Magelicious\Boxy\Api\Data\BoxInterface"
type="Magelicious\Boxy\Model\Box"/>
    <preference for="Magelicious\Boxy\Api\Data\BoxSearchResultsInterface"
type="Magento\Framework\Api\SearchResults" />
    <preference for="Magelicious\Boxy\Api\BoxRepositoryInterface"
type="Magelicious\Boxy\Model\BoxRepository"/>
</config>
```

We then define the `<MAGELICIOUS_DIR>/Boxy/etc/acl.xml` as follows:

```
<config>
  <acl>
    <resources>
      <resource id="Magento_Backend::admin">
        <resource id="Magento_Sales::sales">
          <resource id="Magento_Sales::sales_operation">
            <resource id="Magento_Sales::shipment">
              <resource id="Magelicious_Boxy::box" title="Boxy Box">
                <resource id="Magelicious_Boxy::box_get" title="Get"/>
                <resource id="Magelicious_Boxy::box_search"
title="Search"/>
                <resource id="Magelicious_Boxy::box_save" title="Save"/>
                <resource id="Magelicious_Boxy::box_update"
title="Update"/>
                <resource id="Magelicious_Boxy::box_delete"
title="Delete"/>
              </resource>
```

```
        </resource>
      </resource>
    </resource>
  </resource>
</resources>
    </acl>
</config>
```

We then define the `<MAGELICIOUS_DIR>/Boxy/etc/webapi.xml` as follows:

```
<routes>
  <route url="/V1/boxyBox/:boxId" method="GET">
    <service class="Magelicious\Boxy\Api\BoxRepositoryInterface"
method="getById"/>
    <resources>
      <resource ref="Magelicious_Boxy::box_get"/>
    </resources>
  </route>
  <route url="/V1/boxyBox/search" method="GET">
    <service class="Magelicious\Boxy\Api\BoxRepositoryInterface"
method="getList"/>
    <resources>
      <resource ref="Magelicious_Boxy::box_search"/>
    </resources>
  </route>
  <route url="/V1/boxyBox" method="POST">
    <service class="Magelicious\Boxy\Api\BoxRepositoryInterface"
method="save"/>
    <resources>
      <resource ref="Magelicious_Boxy::box_save"/>
    </resources>
  </route>
  <route url="/V1/boxyBox/:id" method="PUT">
    <service class="Magelicious\Boxy\Api\BoxRepositoryInterface"
method="save"/>
    <resources>
      <resource ref="Magelicious_Boxy::box_update"/>
    </resources>
  </route>
  <route url="/V1/boxyBox/:boxId" method="DELETE">
    <service class="Magelicious\Boxy\Api\BoxRepositoryInterface"
method="deleteById"/>
    <resources>
      <resource ref="Magelicious_Boxy::box_delete"/>
    </resources>
  </route>
</routes>
```

With all these bits in place, our API is now ready. We should now be able to CRUD our way through `Boxy Box` the same way we did with the CMS block. While there certainly is a great deal of *boilerplate code* to go around, our API is now both REST-and SOAP-ready.

Understanding search criteria

The `searchCriteria` parameter of a GET request allows for search results filtering. The key to using it comes down to understanding its structure and the available condition types.

Observing the `\Magento\Framework\Api\SearchCriteriaInterface` interface, and the `Magento\Framework\Api\SearchCriteria` class as its concrete implementation, we can easily conclude the following `search_criteria` structure:

```
"search_criteria": {
    "filter_groups": [],
    "current_page": 1,
    "page_size": 10,
    "sort_orders": []
}
```

Whereas the mandatory `filter_groups` parameter and its structure are shown as follows:

```
"filter_groups": [
  {
    "filters": [
      {
        "field": "fieldOrAttrName",
        "value": "fieldOrAttrValue",
        "condition_type": "eq"
      },
      {
        // Logical OR
      }
    ]
  },
  {
    // Logical AND
  }
],
```

Conditions nested under the individual `filters` key, correspond to the `Logical OR` condition.

The list of `condition_type` values includes:

- `eq`: Equals
- `finset`: A value within a set of values
- `from`: The beginning of a range, must be used with a `to` condition type
- `gt`: Greater than
- `gteq`: Greater than or equal
- `in`: In, the `value` can contain a comma-separated list of values
- `like`: Like, the `value` can contain the SQL wildcard characters
- `lt`: Less than
- `lteq`: Less than or equal to
- `moreq`: More or equal to
- `neq`: Not equal to
- `nin`: Not in; the `value` can contain a comma-separated list of individual values
- `notnull`: Not null
- `null`: Null

Combining these condition types will allow us to filter search results pretty much any way we want.

The optional `sort_orders` parameter and its structure unfold as follows:

```
"sort_orders": [
  {
    "field": "fieldOrAttrName",
    "direction": "ASC"
  }
]
```

The list of direction values includes `ASC` for ascending and `DESC` for descending sort orders.

The `searchCriteria` is seemingly the most complex, yet most powerful aspect of a search API. Understanding how it works is essential for effective querying.

Summary

In this chapter, we have covered valuable web API elements. We learned how to differentiate between types of web API users, and the authentication and methods provided to do so. We also learned how easy it is to create our own APIs with just a few lines of XML. We saw how the `route` definition allows for easy binding between *what comes via an HTTP request to what executes in code*, respecting the access list permissions in the process. The value of building APIs as part of our distributable modules lies in their extensibility. APIs force us to embrace the interface way of thinking, thus allowing others to use and extend our code easily and securely. The `preference` mechanism we introduced in previous chapters, through `di.xml` files, allows others to change the behavior behind the interface easily.

Moving forward, we are going to take a more thorough and rounded look at building and distributing our extensions via Composer and Packagist.

4
Building and Distributing Extensions

At the very start of our journey, we mentioned Magento source files being distributed via three different channels: a *source file archive*, a *Git repository*, and a *Composer repository*. The Composer approach is the preferred way. Whether we are coding a module, library, theme or language component, using the Composer allows for an easy and automated dependency management, which is not possible otherwise. Magento's built-in *Component Manager* can update, uninstall, enable, or disable extensions installed via Composer. This implies sources from Packagist, Magento Marketplace, or other composer sources, as long as they have a `composer.json` file.

Moving forward, we are going to take a closer look at the following topics:

- Building a shipping extension
- Distributing via GitHub
- Distributing via Packagist

 The terms *module, extension, package*, and *component* are used somewhat interchangeably in Magento. While developing, the `module.xml` implies *module* terminology, and `registration.php` implies *component* terminology. However, distributing them via Packagist and Magento marketplace often implies *package* and *extension* terminologies. Magento-wise, to all intents and purposes, they refer to the same thing.

Technical requirements

You will need to have basic knowledge of PHP, OOP, JavaScript, and XML. You will also need Apache, MySQL, and AMPPS installed on your system to execute the codes.

The code files of this chapter can be found on GitHub:
`https://github.com/PacktPublishing/Magento-2-Quick-Start-Guide`.

Check out the following video to see the Code in Action:

`http://bit.ly/2xoS5ms`.

Building a shipping extension

Out of the box, Magento provides several shipping methods of its own. Unlike payment methods, which tend to be less diverse among different web shops, shipping methods are often an area of customization among merchants, which is why building a customized shipping extension is an essential skill for every Magento developer.

There are two types of shipping methods:

- **online**: These shipping methods base their shipping calculation on the shipping service they connect to. The Magento Open Source includes following modules that provide online shipping methods: `Magento_Ups`, `Magento_Usps`, `Magento_Fedex`, `Magento_Dhl`.
- **offline**: These shipping methods do their own shipping calculation, without connecting to an external service. The Magento Open Source includes a built-in `Magento_OfflineShipping` module, which provides **Flat Rate**, **Table Rate**, **Free**, and **Store Pickup** shipping methods.

Let's go ahead and create a Magento shipping extension `Magelicious_RoyalTrek`. The extension assumes an imaginary **RoyalTrek** carrier, with two offline shipping methods: `RoyalTrek Standard` and `RoyalTrek 48h`.

We will start off by defining `<MAGELICIOUS_DIR>/RoyalTrek/registration.php` as follows:

```
\Magento\Framework\Component\ComponentRegistrar::register(
    \Magento\Framework\Component\ComponentRegistrar::MODULE,
    'Magelicious_RoyalTrek',
    __DIR__
);
```

We can then define the `<MAGELICIOUS_DIR>/RoyalTrek/etc/module.xml` as follows:

```
<config>
    <module name="Magelicious_RoyalTrek" setup_version="1.0.0"/>
</config>
```

With these two files in place, Magento should already see our module, when enabled.

We can then go ahead and define the `<MAGELICIOUS_DIR>/RoyalTrek/composer.json` as follows:

```
{
    "name": "magelicious/module-royal-trek",
    "description": "The RoyalTrek shipping",
    "require": {
        "php": "7.0.2|7.0.4|~7.0.6|~7.1.0"
    },
    "type": "magento2-module",
    "version": "1.0.0",
    "license": [
        "OSL-3.0",
        "AFL-3.0"
    ],
    "autoload": {
        "files": [
            "registration.php"
        ],
        "psr-4": {
            "Magelicious\\RoyalTrek\\": ""
        }
    }
}
```

We can then define the `<MAGELICIOUS_DIR>/RoyalTrek/etc/adminhtml/system.xml` as follows:

```
<config>
  <system>
    <section id="carriers">
      <group id="royaltrek">
        <label>Royal Trek Shipping</label>
        <field id="active" type="select">
          <label>Enabled</label>
<source_model>Magento\Config\Model\Config\Source\Yesno</source_model>
        </field>
        <field id="title" type="text">
          <label>Title</label>
        </field>
        <field id="sallowspecific" type="select">
          <label>Ship to Applicable Countries</label>
          <frontend_class>shipping-applicable-country</frontend_class>
<source_model>Magento\Shipping\Model\Config\Source\Allspecificcountries</source_model>
        </field>
```

```
            <field id="specificcountry" type="multiselect">
              <label>Ship to Specific Countries</label>
              <can_be_empty>1</can_be_empty>
    <source_model>Magento\Directory\Model\Config\Source\Country</source_model>
            </field>
            <field id="showmethod" type="select"">
              <label>Show Method if Not Applicable</label>
    <source_model>Magento\Config\Model\Config\Source\Yesno</source_model>
            </field>
            <field id="specificerrmsg" type="textarea">
              <label>Displayed Error Message</label>
            </field>
            <field id="sort_order" type="text">
              <label>Sort Order</label>
              <validate>validate-number validate-zero-or-greater</validate>
            </field>
          </group>
          <!-- todo... -->
        </section>
      </system>
    </config>
```

This sets the general configuration options for our shipping methods. The `sallowspecific, specificcountry, showmethod, specificerrmsg` and, `sort_order` are common configuration elements of each shipping method, as seen by examining the `Magento\Shipping\Model\Carrier\AbstractCarrier` class.

We can then extend the `<MAGELICIOUS_DIR>/RoyalTrek/etc/adminhtml/system.xml` with the following `group`:

```
    <!-- The "RoyalTrek Standard" specific options -->
    <group id="royaltrekstandard">
      <label><![CDATA[The "RoyalTrek Standard" shipping method]]></label>
      <fieldset_css>complex</fieldset_css>
      <field id="title" type="text">
        <label><![CDATA[Title]]></label>
      </field>
      <field id="shippingcost" type="text">
        <label><![CDATA[Shipping Cost]]></label>
        <validate>validate-number validate-zero-or-greater</validate>
      </field>
    </group>
```

We are introducing an additional set of configuration options here, to be used with our `RoyalTrek Standard` method.

So, we then extend the `<MAGELICIOUS_DIR>/RoyalTrek/etc/adminhtml/system.xml` with the following `group`:

```
<!-- The "RoyalTrek 48h" specific options -->
<group id="royaltrek48hr">
  <label><![CDATA[The "RoyalTrek 48h" shipping method]]></label>
  <fieldset_css>complex</fieldset_css>
  <field id="title" type="text">
    <label><![CDATA[Title]]></label>
  </field>
  <field id="shippingcost" type="text">
    <label><![CDATA[Shipping Cost]]></label>
    <validate>validate-number validate-zero-or-greater</validate>
  </field>
</group>
```

We are introducing an additional set of configuration options here, to be used with our `RoyalTrek 48h` method.

We then define the `<MAGELICIOUS_DIR>/RoyalTrek/etc/config.xml` as follows:

```
<config>
  <default>
    <carriers>
      <royaltrek>
        <!-- DEFAULTS HERE -->
      </royaltrek>
    </carriers>
  </default>
</config>
```

The `config > default > carriers > royaltrek` nesting path matches the nesting path of the `system.xml` elements. We then replace the `<!-- DEFAULTS HERE -->` with following:

```
<active>1</active>
<title>Royal Trek Shipping</title>
<sallowspecific>0</sallowspecific>
<showmethod>0</showmethod>
<specificerrmsg>The Royal Trek shipping is not available.</specificerrmsg>
<sort_order>10</sort_order>
<model>Magelicious\RoyalTrek\Model\Carrier\RoyalTrek</model>
<royaltrekstandard>
    <title><![CDATA[RoyalTrek Standard]]></title>
    <shippingcost>4.99</shippingcost>
</royaltrekstandard>
<royaltrek48hr>
```

```
      <title><![CDATA[RoyalTrek 48h]]></title>
      <shippingcost>9.99</shippingcost>
</royaltrek48hr>
```

With this, we can set the default values for each of the configuration options made available via system.xml.

We then define the <MAGELICIOUS_DIR>/Model/Carrier/RoyalTrek.php as follows:

```php
<?php

namespace Magelicious\RoyalTrek\Model\Carrier;

class RoyalTrek extends \Magento\Shipping\Model\Carrier\AbstractCarrier
implements
  \Magento\Shipping\Model\Carrier\CarrierInterface {
    const CARRIER_CODE = 'royaltrek';

    const ROYAL_TREK_STANDARD = 'royaltrekstandard';
    const ROYAL_TREK_48HR = 'royaltrek48hr';

    protected $_code = self::CARRIER_CODE;
    protected $_isFixed = true;
    protected $_rateResultFactory;
    protected $_rateMethodFactory;

    public function __construct(
      \Magento\Framework\App\Config\ScopeConfigInterface $scopeConfig,
      \Magento\Quote\Model\Quote\Address\RateResult\ErrorFactory
$rateErrorFactory,
      \Psr\Log\LoggerInterface $logger,
      \Magento\Shipping\Model\Rate\ResultFactory $rateResultFactory,
      \Magento\Quote\Model\Quote\Address\RateResult\MethodFactory
$rateMethodFactory,
      array $data = []
    ) {
      $this->_rateResultFactory = $rateResultFactory;
      $this->_rateMethodFactory = $rateMethodFactory;
      parent::__construct($scopeConfig, $rateErrorFactory, $logger, $data);
    }

    public function
collectRates(\Magento\Quote\Model\Quote\Address\RateRequest $request) {
      if (!$this->getConfigFlag('active')) {
        return false;
      }

      $result = $this->_rateResultFactory->create();
```

```
    // Todo...
    return $result;
  }

  public function getAllowedMethods() {
    return [
      self::ROYAL_TREK_STANDARD =>
$this->getConfigData(self::ROYAL_TREK_STANDARD . '/title'),
      self::ROYAL_TREK_48HR => $this->getConfigData(self::ROYAL_TREK_48HR .
'/title'),
    ];
  }

  private function getMethodTitle($method) {
    return $this->getConfigData($method . '/title');
  }

  private function getMethodPrice($method) {
    return $this->getMethodCost($method);
  }
  private function getMethodCost($method) {
    return $this->getConfigData($method . '/shippingcost');
  }
}
```

The basic implementation of the `Magelicious\RoyalTrek\Model\Carrier\RoyalTrek` class is highly determined by the implementation of its underlying `Magento\Shipping\Model\Carrier\AbstractCarrier` parent class and `Magento\Shipping\Model\Carrier\CarrierInterface` interface. The bare minimum implies setting up the `$_code` value and implementing the `collectRates` method. The `$_code` value is an extremely important bit of information here. We need to make sure it is unique among all of the enabled shipping extensions. The `collectRates` method is where the actual shipping calculation implementation happens.

Let's go ahead and extend the `<MAGELICIOUS_DIR>/Model/Carrier/RoyalTrek.php` with the following:

```
$method = $this->_rateMethodFactory->create();
$method->setCarrier($this->_code);
$method->setCarrierTitle($this->getConfigData('title'));
$method->setMethod(self::ROYAL_TREK_STANDARD);
$method->setMethodTitle($this->getMethodTitle($method->getMethod()));
$method->setPrice($this->getMethodPrice($method->getMethod()));
$method->setCost($this->getMethodCost($method->getMethod()));
$method->setErrorMessage(__('The %1 method error message here.'));
$result->append($method);
```

Using the factory, we can create an instance of
`Magento\Quote\Model\Quote\Address\RateResult\Method`. This is the individual shipping method that we wish to make available as a choice during checkout. We then set the required values for the carrier: method, price, cost, and possible error message. With our `royaltrekstandard` method properly set, we finally pass it on to the `$result` object.

Let's further extend the `<MAGELICIOUS_DIR>/Model/Carrier/RoyalTrek.php` with the following:

```
$method = $this->_rateMethodFactory->create();
$method->setCarrier($this->_code);
$method->setCarrierTitle($this->getConfigData('title'));
$method->setMethod(self::ROYAL_TREK_48HR);
$method->setMethodTitle($this->getMethodTitle($method->getMethod()));
$method->setPrice($this->getMethodPrice($method->getMethod()));
$method->setCost($this->getMethodCost($method->getMethod()));
$method->setErrorMessage(__('The %1 method error message here.'));
$result->append($method);
```

Much like with the previous example, here we should add our `royaltrek48hr` to the `$result` object.

The end result should bring forth our two **RoyalTrek** shipping methods to the storefront checkout **Shipping** step, as follows:

Shipping Methods		
$5.00	Fixed	Flat Rate
$4.99	RoyalTrek Standard	Royal Trek Shipping
$9.99	RoyalTrek 48h	Royal Trek Shipping

The **Order Summary** section of the **Review & Payments** step should also reflect on the method selected in the **Shipping** step, as follows:

Order Summary

Cart Subtotal Excl. Tax	$19.99
Cart Subtotal Incl. Tax	$22.99
Shipping Excl. Tax Royal Trek Shipping - RoyalTrek 48h	$9.99
Shipping Incl. Tax Royal Trek Shipping - RoyalTrek 48h	$9.99
Tax	$3.00 ⌄
Order Total	**$32.98**
1 Item in Cart	⌄

Likewise, the admin **Create New Order** screens should also show our **RoyalTrek** shipping methods as follows:

Shipping Method *

Flat Rate

◯ Fixed - **$5.00**

Royal Trek Shipping

◯ RoyalTrek Standard - **$4.99**

◯ RoyalTrek 48h - **$9.99**

Finally, the successfully made order should reflect the **RoyalTrek 48h** shipping method selection in its new order email, and the customer's **My Account** area, as follows:

Shipping Method

Royal Trek Shipping - RoyalTrek 48h

With our shipping methods confirmed as working, let's go ahead and look for a way of distributing it.

Distributing via GitHub

By default, the Packagist repository is the only registered repository in Composer. We can add more repositories to our Magento project by declaring them in `composer.json`. This way we get to register our own `git` repository as a source of packages, as follows:

```
composer config repositories.magelicious-royal-trek git
git@github.com:foggyline/Magelicious_RoyalTrek.git
```

This command results in the modified `composer.json` file, with the `repositories` key amended as follows:

```
"repositories": {
    "0": {
        "type": "composer",
        "url": "https://repo.magento.com/"
    },
    "magelicious-royal-trek": {
        "type": "git",
        "url": "git@github.com:foggyline/Magelicious_RoyalTrek.git"
    }
},
```

We can see our `magelicious-royal-trek` entry added in there. The `git` value used for the `type` key tells the Composer we are using the `git` repository, located at the URL provided via the `url` key. The `composer` and `git` are not the only two values supported for the `type`. The actual `type` value could have easily been any other type of supported version control system:

- Git (`git-scm.com`)
- Subversion (`subversion.apache.org`)
- Mercurial (`mercurial-scm.org`)
- Fossil (`fossil-scm.org`)

We could also have simply used the `vcs` value for the `type` key, and relied on Composer's VCS driver to automatically detect the type based `url` value.

If we now execute `composer require magelicious/royal-trek:dev-master`, Composer will install our shipping module. While this new repositories approach works well, it is somewhat more suited for distributing private Magento extensions. Whenever we wish to distribute our extension publicly, a Packagist is a more convenient way to go.

Distributing via Packagist

Packagist is a free online repository service for Composer packages. We can use it to easily distribute our free Magento modules. The fact that Packagist is a default Composer repository, makes it the de facto repository for any Composer user. This is why having our free Magento modules available via Packagist is a preferred way of distribution.

Pushing our Magento module to Packagist is quite easy. Assuming we have our account created, we should start by clicking on the **Submit** button, which will land us on the following screen:

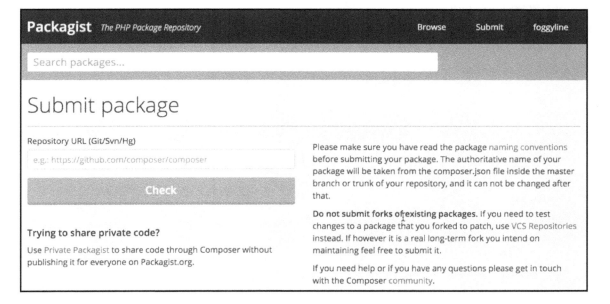

We need to provide a link to our Git repository here, and click the **Check** button, followed by the **Submit** button, if the valid repository was found. This should create our package, as per the following screen:

The Packagist says that our created package is now available for use via the `composer require magelicious/module-royal-trek` command. However, running this command now would be likely to give us the following error:

```
[InvalidArgumentException]
Could not find a matching version of package magelicious/module-royal-trek.
Check the package spelling, your version constraint and that the package is
available in a stability which matches your minimum-stability (stable).
```

Notice the `dev-master` label on our Packagist screen. Our branches automatically appear as *dev* versions in Packagist. Therefore, we can use the `composer require magelicious/module-royal-trek:dev-master` command to fetch the package. To change that, we need to specifically tag our `git` commits, as follows:

```
git add .
git commit -a -m 'The RoyalTrek shipping module, first version.'
git tag 1.0.0
git push origin 1.0.0
```

Once we have done that, we can go back to the Packagist package screen and hit the **Update** button. This should now show our **1.0.0** version:

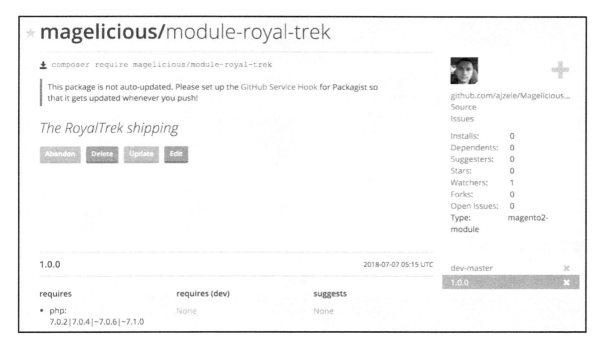

If we specify a version when requiring the package, Composer fetches the latest tagged version from the `master`. For example, `composer require magelicious/module-royal-trek:2.4.x` takes the latest `2.4` tagged version from the `master` branch.

When it comes to versioning, it is worth noting that `setup_version` found in `module.xml`, and `version` found in `composer.json` are two different types of versioning. Magento refers to them as *marketing version* and *composer version*. Marketing version might be thought of as something the merchant interacts with, while Composer version is something that developers interact with. The `Magento_Catalog` module, for example, uses the `2.2.4` marketing version for marketing, whereas its Composer version is `102.0.4`. This is not to say that we cannot use the same versioning for both, as long as we remember that the `setup_version`, found in `module.xml`, is what drives our setup scripts.

Distributing future new versions of our `Magelicious_RoyalTrek` module would, therefore, come down to:

1. Bumping up the `setup_version` found in `module.xml`
2. Bumping up the `version` found in `composer.json`
3. Addressing any necessary Magento setup scripts
4. Committing our changes to Git, with proper version tagging
5. Making sure the **Update** is triggered on the Packagist screen of our module edit screen

 Using the Packagist's service hook we can ensure that our package will always be updated automatically. See `https://packagist.org/about#how-to-update-packages` for more information.

Summary

In this chapter, we learned how to create a simple shipping module. We saw how easy it is to add specific shipping calculations as part of offline shipping methods. We then packaged this module and distributed it via Packagist. This made it easy for the end consumer to use our module, with just a few simple console commands. Likewise, any future updates to our module should be frictionless for the end consumer, as composer can easily handle those via simple `composer update` commands.

Moving forward, we are going to take a look at some of the specifics of Magento admin area development.

5
Developing for Admin

At the very beginning of our journey, back in Chapter 1, *Understanding Magento Architecture*, we mentioned how Magento consists of different *areas*. Developing for Magento admin implies developing for the adminhtml area. While the majority of code is applicable across different areas, there are certain subtle differences. Unlike frontend which is mostly built via HTML (.phtml, .html), the Magento adminhtml area is mostly built via *UI components* which are referenced, stacked, and configured through .xml files. This is not to say that the same components cannot be used both for frontend and admin, because all UI components can be configured for both of these areas; we just need to configure styles manually for components on the frontend.

There are two basic UI components in Magento: listing and form. The rest are secondary components, which serve as extensions of basic components: listingToolbar, columns, filters, column, form, and field.

To get a better understanding of the adminhtml area, we are going to build a Magelicious_Minventory module, using some of these components. The idea behind the module is to provide a custom listing interface for a limited set of users, where they can easily bump up the product stock in certain increments without ever getting access to other areas of the Magento admin.

Our work here will consist of two major parts:

- Using the listing component
- Using the form component

To keep things compact, we will use the <MODULE_DIR> to reference the MAGELICIOUS_DIR>/Minventory directory.

Technical requirements

You will need to have basic knowledge of PHP, OOP, JavaScript, and XML. You will also need Apache, MySQL, and AMPPS installed on your system to execute the codes.

The code files of this chapter can be found on GitHub:
`https://github.com/PacktPublishing/Magento-2-Quick-Start-Guide`.

Check out the following video to see the Code in Action:

`http://bit.ly/2xuoFDL`.

Using the listing component

The `listing` is a basic component responsible for rendering grids, lists, and tiles, providing filtering, pagination, sorting, and other features. The `listingElements` group referenced in the `vendor/magento/module-ui/etc/ui_configuration.xsd` file provides a nice list of both primary and secondary *listing* components:

actions	component	file	massaction	select
actionsColumn	container	filters	modal	selectionsColumn
bookmark	dataSource	form	multiline	tab
boolean	dataProvider	hidden	multiselect	text
button	date	htmlContent	nav	textarea
checkbox	dynamicRows	input	number	wysiwyg
checkboxset	email	insertForm	paging	
column	exportButton	insertListing	price	
columns	field	listing	range	
columnsControls	fieldset	listingToolbar	radioset	

The key to using all of these components is to understand:

- *What parameters individual components accept*—further revealed by definitions found in the `vendor/magento/moduleui/view/base/ui_component/etc/` definition directory
- *What child components individual components accept*—for example, the `email` component cannot be nested within the `dataProvider` component

Moving forward, we will use the `listing` component, and a few of its *secondary* components to create the **Micro Inventory** screen as shown:

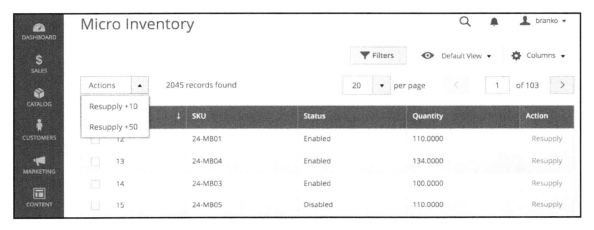

The grid itself is to consist of **ID**, **SKU**, **Status**, **Quantity**, and **Action** columns. The **Resupply** action will trigger redirection to a custom **Stock Resupply** screen, which we will address in the next section. The **Actions** selector in the upper left corner is to consist of two custom actions, allowing for fixed product stock increases.

Assuming we have defined our basic `registration.php`, `composer.json`, and `etc/module.xml` files, we can start dealing with the specifics of our module.

Let's start by defining the `<MODULE_DIR>/etc/acl.xml` as follows:

```
<config>
  <acl>
    <resources>
      <resource id="Magento_Backend::admin">
        <resource id="Magento_Catalog::catalog">
          <resource id="Magento_Catalog::catalog_inventory">
            <resource id="Magelicious_Minventory::minventory" title="Micro
Inventory"/>
          </resource>
        </resource>
      </resource>
    </resources>
  </acl>
</config>
```

The requirement of our module was to *provide a custom listing interface for a limited set of users.* The *access list* entry, later referenced by our admin controller, ensures just that. The choice to nest our `Magelicious_Minventory::minventory` as a child of `Magento_Catalog::catalog_inventory` is based merely on logical grouping, as our module deals with inventory stock. We should now be able to see **Micro Inventory** under **Roles Resources** as shown:

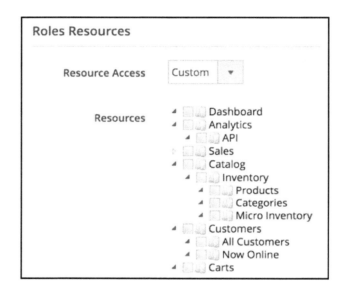

We then define the `<MODULE_DIR>/etc/adminhtml/routes.xml` as follows:

```
<config>
  <router id="admin">
    <route id="minventory" frontName="minventory">
      <module name="Magelicious_Minventory"/>
    </route>
  </router>
</config>
```

This will allow us to access our controller actions later on via `http://magelicious.loc/index.php/<admin>/minventory/<controller>/<action>` links.

We then define the `<MODULE_DIR>/etc/adminhtml/menu.xml` as follows:

```
<config>
  <menu>
    <add id="Magelicious_Minventory::minventory"
      title="Micro Inventory" translate="title"
      module="Magelicious_Minventory" sortOrder="100"
      parent="Magento_Catalog::inventory"
      action="minventory/product/index"
      resource="Magelicious_Minventory::minventory"/>
  </menu>
</config>
```

This positions our **Micro Inventory** menu right under the main **Catalog | CATALOGUE** menu, as shown:

When clicked, the menu's `minventory/product/index` action will throw us at `<MODULE_DIR>/Controller/Adminhtml/Product/Index.php`, which will be addressed later on.

We then define the `<MODULE_DIR>/Model/Resupply.php` as follows:

```
namespace Magelicious\Minventory\Model;

class Resupply
{
  protected $productRepository;
  protected $collectionFactory;
  protected $stockRegistry;

  public function __construct(
    \Magento\Catalog\Api\ProductRepositoryInterface $productRepository,
    \Magento\Catalog\Model\ResourceModel\Product\CollectionFactory
```

```
$collectionFactory,
    \Magento\CatalogInventory\Api\StockRegistryInterface $stockRegistry
)
{
    $this->productRepository = $productRepository;
    $this->collectionFactory = $collectionFactory;
    $this->stockRegistry = $stockRegistry;
}

public function resupply($productId, $qty)
{
    $product = $this->productRepository->getById($productId);
    $stockItem =
$this->stockRegistry->getStockItemBySku($product->getSku());
    $stockItem->setQty($stockItem->getQty() + $qty);
    $stockItem->setIsInStock((bool)$stockItem->getQty());
    $this->stockRegistry->updateStockItemBySku($product->getSku(),
$stockItem);
    }}
```

This class will serve as a centralized stock updater for our module, which will be updating stock from the **Actions** *selector* found on the **Micro Inventory** screen, as well as from the **Save** button action triggered on the **Stock Resupply** screen.

We then define the <MODULE_DIR>/Controller/Adminhtml/Product.php as follows:

```
namespace Magelicious\Minventory\Controller\Adminhtml;

abstract class Product extends \Magento\Backend\App\Action
{
    const ADMIN_RESOURCE = 'Magelicious_Minventory::minventory';
}
```

This is our *controller* file, the parent of the *controller actions* that we will soon define. We set the value of its ADMIN_RESOURCE constant to that defined in our acl.xml file. This will empower our controller to only allow access to users with proper resource roles.

We then define the <MODULE_DIR>/Controller/Adminhtml/Product/Index.php as follows:

```
namespace Magelicious\Minventory\Controller\Adminhtml\Product;

use \Magento\Framework\Controller\ResultFactory;

class Index extends \Magelicious\Minventory\Controller\Adminhtml\Product
{
    public function execute()
```

```
    {
      $resultPage = $this->resultFactory->create(ResultFactory::TYPE_PAGE);
      $resultPage->getConfig()->getTitle()->prepend((__('Micro Inventory')));
      return $resultPage;
    }
}
```

This controller action does not really do anything special. Aside from setting up the screen title, it merely provides a *mechanism* for loading the `minventory_product_index.xml` that we will address later on.

We then define the
`<MODULE_DIR>/Controller/Adminhtml/Product/MassResupply.php` as follows:

```
namespace Magelicious\Minventory\Controller\Adminhtml\Product;

use \Magento\Framework\Controller\ResultFactory;

class MassResupply extends
\Magelicious\Minventory\Controller\Adminhtml\Product
{
  protected $filter;
  protected $collectionFactory;
  protected $resupply;

  public function __construct(
    \Magento\Backend\App\Action\Context $context,
    \Magento\Ui\Component\MassAction\Filter $filter,
    \Magento\Catalog\Model\ResourceModel\Product\CollectionFactory
$collectionFactory,
    \Magelicious\Minventory\Model\Resupply $resupply
  )
  {
    parent::__construct($context);
    $this->filter = $filter;
    $this->collectionFactory = $collectionFactory;
    $this->resupply = $resupply;
  }

  public function execute()
  {
    $redirectResult =
$this->resultFactory->create(ResultFactory::TYPE_REDIRECT);
    $qty = $this->getRequest()->getParam('qty');
    $collection =
$this->filter->getCollection($this->collectionFactory->create());

    $productResupplied = 0;
```

```
    foreach ($collection->getItems() as $product) {
      $this->resupply->resupply($product->getId(), $qty);
      $productResupplied++;
    }

    $this->messageManager->addSuccessMessage(__('A total of %1 record(s)
  have been resupplied.', $productResupplied));

    return $redirectResult->setPath('minventory/product/index');
  }
}
```

This controller action will be triggered by the **Resupply +10** and **Resupply +50** actions from the **Micro Inventory** screen. We can see it using the `Magento\Ui\Component\MassAction\Filter` to process the *mass select* options, binding them internally to product collection in order to filter products we have selected properly.

We then define the `<MODULE_DIR>/view/adminhtml/layout/minventory_product_index.xml` as follows:

```
<page>
  <update handle="styles"/>
  <body>
    <referenceContainer name="content">
      <uiComponent name="minventory_listing"/>
    </referenceContainer>
  </body>
</page>
```

This is the layout file that gets triggered when we land on `<MODULE_DIR>/Controller/Adminhtml/Product/Index.php`. The name of the file matches the `<routeName>/<controllerName>/<controllerActionName>` path. The actual layout here merely references the `content` container, to which it adds the `minventory_listing` component using the `uiComponent` element.

We then define the `<MODULE_DIR>/view/adminhtml/ui_component/minventory_listing.xml` as follows:

```
<listing>
    <argument name="data" xsi:type="array">
        <item name="js_config" xsi:type="array">
            <item name="provider"
xsi:type="string">minventory_listing.minventory_listing_data_source</item>
        </item>
```

```
        </argument>
        <settings>
            <spinner>minventory_columns</spinner>
            <deps>
                <dep>minventory_listing.minventory_listing_data_source</dep>
            </deps>
        </settings>
        <!-- dataSource -->
        <!-- listingToolbar -->
        <!-- columns -->
    </listing>
```

This is our **listing** component. The
`minventory_listing.minventory_listing_data_source` is our data source defined
under the `dataSource` element.

We then modify the `minventory_listing.xml` by replacing the `<!-- dataSource -->`
with the following:

```
<dataSource name="minventory_listing_data_source"
component="Magento_Ui/js/grid/provider">
    <settings>
        <storageConfig>
            <param name="indexField" xsi:type="string">entity_id</param>
        </storageConfig>
        <updateUrl path="mui/index/render"/>
    </settings>
    <dataProvider
class="Magelicious\Minventory\Ui\DataProvider\Product\ProductDataProvider"
name="minventory_listing_data_source">
        <settings>
            <requestFieldName>id</requestFieldName>
            <primaryFieldName>entity_id</primaryFieldName>
        </settings>
    </dataProvider>
</dataSource>
```

The most important part of the `dataSource` component is its `dataProvider`. We set its
value to
`Magelicious\Minventory\Ui\DataProvider\Product\ProductDataProvider`. The
`requestFieldName` and `primaryFieldName` are not really that important in our case, as
we are not really operating with full CRUD on the product entity, since we are merely
focusing on updating the quantity through a few lines of custom code. Still, the component
itself requires a certain minimal configuration, so we use what we would normally use for a
product entity, but these can really be any values found on an entity.

We then define the
`<MODULE_DIR>/Ui/DataProvider/Product/ProductDataProvider.php` as follows:

```
class ProductDataProvider extends
\Magento\Ui\DataProvider\AbstractDataProvider {
    protected $collection;

    public function __construct(
        string $name,
        string $primaryFieldName,
        string $requestFieldName,
        \Magento\Catalog\Model\ResourceModel\Product\CollectionFactory
$collectionFactory,
        array $meta = [],
        array $data = []
    ) {
        parent::__construct(
            $name,
            $primaryFieldName,
            $requestFieldName,
            $meta,
            $data
        );
        $this->collection = $collectionFactory->create();
    }

    public function getData() {
        if (!$this->getCollection()->isLoaded()) {
            $this->getCollection()->load();
        }
        $items = $this->getCollection()->toArray();
        return [
            'totalRecords' => $this->getCollection()->getSize(),
            'items' => array_values($items),
        ];
    }
}
```

The collection property is set mandatorily by the parent
`Magento\Ui\DataProvider\AbstractDataProvider`, so we have to set its value to
some kind of collection. Since we are working with products, it only makes sense to set it to
an existing `Magento\Catalog\Model\ResourceModel\Product\Collection`, thus
avoiding creating our own collection. The key method for our listing component is
`getData`. This method feeds the listing component with the number of records in the data
collection, as well as the data collection itself.

We then extend the `ProductDataProvider.php` with the following:

```
protected function joinQty() {
  if ($this->getCollection()) {
    $this->getCollection()->joinField(
      'qty',
      'cataloginventory_stock_item',
      'qty',
      'product_id=entity_id'
    );
  }
}
```

The `qty` field is not part of the default products collection, so we have to join the `qty` information from the `cataloginventory_stock_item` table to it. We must make sure to call this method before our collection is loaded.

We then modify the `minventory_listing.xml` by replacing the `<!-- listingToolbar -->` with the following:

```
<listingToolbar name="listing_top">
  <bookmark name="bookmarks"/>
  <columnsControls name="columns_controls"/>
  <filters name="listing_filters" />
  <paging name="listing_paging"/>
  <-- massaction -->
</listingToolbar>
```

The `listingToolbar` component is essentially a container for the listing-related elements like paging, mass actions, filters, and bookmarks. The `bookmark` component stores the active and changed states of data grids. The `paging` component provides navigation through the pages of the collection, otherwise, we would be forced to view the entire collection at once, which would not really be a performance-efficient approach. The `filters` component is responsible for rendering filters' interfaces and applying the actual filtering. This includes the states of filters, columns' positions, applied sorting, pagination, and so on.

The `columnsControls` component allows us to modify the visibility of the listing columns, shown as follows:

The possibility of filtering by `Store View`, as shown in the preceding screenshot, is easily added by modifying the `minventory_listing.xml` as follows:

```
<filters name="listing_filters">
  <filterSelect name="store_id" provider="${ $.parentName }">
    <settings>
      <options
class="Magento\Store\Ui\Component\Listing\Column\Store\Options"/>
      <caption translate="true">All Store Views</caption>
      <label translate="true">Store View</label>
      <dataScope>store_id</dataScope>
    </settings>
  </filterSelect>
</filters>
```

Here we used the `filterSelect` component, with the `Magento\Store\Ui\Component\Listing\Column\Store\Options` class passed as an `options` parameter. This shows how easy it is to combine various components and to pull data from PHP classes.

Let's modify the `minventory_listing.xml` further by replacing the `<-- massaction -->` with the following:

```
<massaction name="listing_massaction" component="Magento_Ui/js/grid/tree-massactions">
  <action name="resupply">
    <settings>
      <type>resupply</type>
      <label translate="true">Resupply</label>
      <actions>
```

```
            <action name="0">
              <type>resupply_10</type>
              <label translate="true">Resupply +10</label>
              <url path="minventory/product/massResupply">
                <param name="qty">10</param>
              </url>
            </action>
            <action name="1">
              <type>resupply_50</type>
              <label translate="true">Resupply +50</label>
              <url path="minventory/product/massResupply">
                <param name="qty">50</param>
              </url>
            </action>
          </actions>
        </settings>
      </action>
    </massaction>
```

Using the action component, we define the **Resupply +10** and **Resupply +50** actions used in the scope of the massaction component.

We then modify the minventory_listing.xml by replacing the <!-- columns --> with the following:

```
<columns name="minventory_columns"
class="Magento\Catalog\Ui\Component\Listing\Columns">
  <settings>
    <childDefaults>
      <param name="fieldAction" xsi:type="array">
        <item name="provider"
xsi:type="string">minventory_listing.minventory_listing.minventory_columns.
actions</item>
        <item name="target" xsi:type="string">applyAction</item>
        <item name="params" xsi:type="array">
          <item name="0" xsi:type="string">resupply</item>
          <item name="1" xsi:type="string">${ $.$data.rowIndex }</item>
        </item>
      </param>
    </childDefaults>
  </settings>
  <!-- columns#2 -->
</columns>
```

The `columns` component definition, along with its child components, is likely to take the biggest chunk of our `listing` configuration. This is where we add our *selection columns*, regular *columns*, and *action columns*.

To demonstrate that further, we replace the `<!-- columns#2 -->` with the following:

```
<selectionsColumn name="ids" sortOrder="0">
  <settings>
    <indexField>entity_id</indexField>
  </settings>
</selectionsColumn>
<column name="entity_id" sortOrder="10">
  <settings>
    <filter>textRange</filter>
    <label translate="true">ID</label>
    <sorting>asc</sorting>
  </settings>
</column>
<column name="sku" sortOrder="20">
  <settings>
    <filter>text</filter>
    <label translate="true">SKU</label>
  </settings>
</column>
<column name="qty" sortOrder="30">
  <settings>
    <addField>true</addField>
    <filter>textRange</filter>
    <label translate="true">Quantity</label>
  </settings>
</column>
<actionsColumn name="resupply"
class="Magelicious\Minventory\Ui\Component\Listing\Columns\Resupply"
sortOrder="40">
  <settings>
    <indexField>entity_id</indexField>
  </settings>
</actionsColumn>
```

The `actionsColumn` points to a custom `Magelicious\Minventory\Ui\Component\Listing\Columns\Resupply` class, which we define under `<MODULE_DIR>/Ui/Component/Listing/Columns/Resupply.php` as follows:

```
class Resupply extends \Magento\Ui\Component\Listing\Columns\Column {
  protected $urlBuilder;
```

```
public function __construct(
  \Magento\Framework\View\Element\UiComponent\ContextInterface $context,
  \Magento\Framework\View\Element\UiComponentFactory $uiComponentFactory,
  \Magento\Framework\UrlInterface $urlBuilder,
  array $components = [],
  array $data = []
) {
  $this->urlBuilder = $urlBuilder;
  parent::__construct($context, $uiComponentFactory, $components, $data);
}

public function prepareDataSource(array $dataSource) {
  if (isset($dataSource['data']['items'])) {
    $storeId = $this->context->getFilterParam('store_id');

    foreach ($dataSource['data']['items'] as &$item) {
      $item[$this->getData('name')]['resupply'] = [
        'href' => $this->urlBuilder->getUrl(
          'minventory/product/resupply',
          ['id' => $item['entity_id'], 'store' => $storeId]
        ),
        'label' => __('Resupply'),
        'hidden' => false,
      ];
    }
  }
  return $dataSource;
}
}
```

The `prepareDataSource` method is where we inject our modifications. We traverse the `$dataSource['data']['items']` structure until we come across our column, and then modify it accordingly with a proper `href` value. This, in turn, renders our `resupply` actions column as per the **Micro Inventory** screen.

With the **Micro Inventory** screen now sorted via the `listing` component, let's shift our focus onto the **Stock Resupply** screen built via the `form` component.

Using the form component

The form is a basic component responsible for performing CRUD operations on an entity. The listingElements group referenced under vendor/magento/module-ui/etc/ui_configuration.xsd file provides a nice list of both primary and secondary form components:

bookmark	dataProvider	fileUploader	massaction	range
boolean	date	form	modal	radioset
button	dynamicRows	hidden	multiline	select
checkbox	email	htmlContent	multiselect	tab
checkboxset	exportButton	input	nav	text
component	field	insertForm	number	textarea
container	fieldset	insertListing	paging	wysiwyg
dataSource	file	listing	price	

Moving forward, we will use the form component, and a few of its *secondary* components to create the **Stock Resupply** screen as shown:

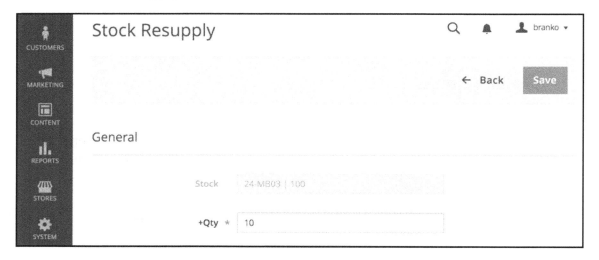

The form itself is to consist of **Stock** and **+Qty** fields. The **Stock** field will be a read-only field consisting of an *SKU + current qty* string. The **Back** button will take us back to the **Micro Inventory** listing, whereas the **Save** button will post the form to a special Resupply controller action, which will then increase the stock by a given **+Qty** amount. The **Actions** selector in the upper left corner is to consist of two custom actions, allowing for fixed product stock increases.

We start off by defining the
<MODULE_DIR>/Controller/Adminhtml/Product/Resupply.php as follows:

```php
use \Magento\Framework\Controller\ResultFactory;
class Resupply extends \Magelicious\Minventory\Controller\Adminhtml\Product
{
  protected $stockRegistry;
  protected $productRepository;
  protected $resupply;

  public function __construct(
    \Magento\Backend\App\Action\Context $context,
    \Magento\Catalog\Api\ProductRepositoryInterface $productRepository,
    \Magento\CatalogInventory\Api\StockRegistryInterface $stockRegistry,
    \Magelicious\Minventory\Model\Resupply $resupply
  ) {
    parent::__construct($context);
    $this->productRepository = $productRepository;
    $this->stockRegistry = $stockRegistry;
    $this->resupply = $resupply;
  }

  public function execute() {
    if ($this->getRequest()->isPost()) {
      $this->resupply->resupply(
        $this->getRequest()->getParam('id'),
        $_POST['minventory_product']['qty']
      );
      $this->messageManager->addSuccessMessage(__('Successfully
resupplied'));
      $redirectResult =
$this->resultFactory->create(ResultFactory::TYPE_REDIRECT);
      return $redirectResult->setPath('minventory/product/index');
    } else {
      $resultPage = $this->resultFactory->create(ResultFactory::TYPE_PAGE);
      $resultPage->getConfig()->getTitle()->prepend((__('Stock
Resupply')));
      return $resultPage;
    }
  }
}
```

Given the simplicity of our form, using the isPost() check on the request object, we allow ourselves to use the same controller action for rendering the **Stock Resupply** screen, as well as submitting the save action to it.

With controller action in place, we then define the
`<MODULE_DIR>/view/adminhtml/layout/minventory_product_resupply.xml` as
follows:

```xml
<page>
  <update handle="styles"/>
  <body>
    <referenceContainer name="content">
      <uiComponent name="minventory_resupply_form"/>
    </referenceContainer>
  </body>
</page>
```

Much like with the form listing, this layout file merely calls the
`minventory_resupply_form` component, which is where all our visual elements of the
Stock Resupply screen reside.

We then define the
`<MODULE_DIR>/view/adminhtml/ui_component/minventory_resupply_form.xml` as
follows:

```xml
<form>
  <argument name="data" xsi:type="array">
    <item name="js_config" xsi:type="array">
      <item name="provider"
xsi:type="string">minventory_resupply_form.minventory_resupply_form_data_so
urce</item>
      <item name="deps"
xsi:type="string">minventory_resupply_form.minventory_resupply_form_data_so
urce</item>
    </item>
    <item name="layout" xsi:type="array">
      <item name="type" xsi:type="string">tabs</item>
    </item>
  </argument>
  <settings>
    <buttons>
      <button name="save"
class="Magelicious\Minventory\Block\Adminhtml\Product\Edit\Button\Save"/>
      <button name="back"
class="Magelicious\Minventory\Block\Adminhtml\Product\Edit\Button\Back"/>
    </buttons>
  </settings>
  <!-- dataSource -->
  <!-- fieldset -->
</form>
```

Much like the `listing` component, the `form` component also requires a *data provider*.

We then modify the `minventory_resupply_form.xml` by replacing the `<!--dataSource -->` with following:

```
<dataSource name="minventory_resupply_form_data_source">
  <argument name="data" xsi:type="array">
    <item name="js_config" xsi:type="array">
      <item name="component"
xsi:type="string">Magento_Ui/js/form/provider</item>
    </item>
  </argument>
  <dataProvider
class="Magelicious\Minventory\Ui\DataProvider\Product\Form\ProductDataProvi
der" name="minventory_resupply_form_data_source">
    <settings>
      <requestFieldName>id</requestFieldName>
      <primaryFieldName>entity_id</primaryFieldName>
    </settings>
  </dataProvider>
</dataSource>
```

Here we set the data provider, which points to our custom class, `Magelicious\Minventory\Ui\DataProvider\Product\Form\ProductDataProvider`.

We further modify the `minventory_resupply_form.xml` by replacing the `<!--fieldset -->` with the following:

```
<fieldset name="minventory_product">
  <argument name="data" xsi:type="array">
    <item name="config" xsi:type="array">
      <item name="label" xsi:type="string" translate="true">General</item>
    </item>
  </argument>
  <field name="stock">
    <argument name="data" xsi:type="array">
      <item name="config" xsi:type="array">
        <item name="label" xsi:type="string">Stock</item>
        <item name="visible" xsi:type="boolean">true</item>
        <item name="dataType" xsi:type="string">text</item>
        <item name="formElement" xsi:type="string">input</item>
        <item name="disabled" xsi:type="string">true</item>
      </item>
    </argument>
  </field>
  <field name="qty">
```

```
        <argument name="data" xsi:type="array">
          <item name="config" xsi:type="array">
            <item name="label" xsi:type="string">+Qty</item>
            <item name="visible" xsi:type="boolean">true</item>
            <item name="dataType" xsi:type="string">text</item>
            <item name="formElement" xsi:type="string">input</item>
            <item name="focused" xsi:type="string">true</item>
            <item name="validation" xsi:type="array">
              <item name="required-entry" xsi:type="boolean">true</item>
              <item name="validate-zero-or-greater"
  xsi:type="boolean">true</item>
            </item>
          </item>
        </argument>
      </field>
  </fieldset>
```

Here we defined `fieldset` with a **General** title, and two fields: `stock` and `qty`. The `stock` field was defined as *disabled*, as its purpose will be merely to merge the `<SKU>` | `<qty>` values for informational purposes. The structure of the individual field definition might seem overwhelming at first, but we can easily determine available arguments by observing the `<component name="column"` definition under the `<MAGENTO_DIR>/module-ui/view/base/ui_component/etc/definition.map.xml`.

We then define `<MODULE_DIR>/Ui/DataProvider/Product/Form/ProductDataProvider.php` as follows:

```
class ProductDataProvider extends
\Magento\Ui\DataProvider\AbstractDataProvider {
  protected $loadedData;
  protected $productRepository;
  protected $stockRegistry;
  protected $request;

  public function __construct(
    string $name,
    string $primaryFieldName,
    string $requestFieldName,
    \Magento\Catalog\Model\ResourceModel\Product\CollectionFactory
$collectionFactory,
    \Magento\Catalog\Api\ProductRepositoryInterface $productRepository,
    \Magento\CatalogInventory\Api\StockRegistryInterface $stockRegistry,
    \Magento\Framework\App\RequestInterface $request,
    array $meta = [], array $data = []
  ) {
    parent::__construct($name, $primaryFieldName, $requestFieldName, $meta,
```

```
$data);
    $this->collection = $collectionFactory->create();
    $this->productRepository = $productRepository;
    $this->stockRegistry = $stockRegistry;
    $this->request = $request;
  }

  public function getData() {
    if (isset($this->loadedData)) {
      return $this->loadedData;
    }
    $id = $this->request->getParam('id');
    $product = $this->productRepository->getById($id);
    $stockItem =
$this->stockRegistry->getStockItemBySku($product->getSku());
    $this->loadedData[$product->getId()]['minventory_product'] = [
      'stock' => __('%1 | %2', $product->getSku(), $stockItem->getQty()),
      'qty' => 10
    ];
    return $this->loadedData;
  }
}
```

Our data provider is expected to implement the getData method. This returns an array of data that *feeds the form* with proper values. The structure of the array might be difficult to grasp at first, so it helps to gloss over some of Magento's data providers. The stock and qty entries here will provide values for the fields defined via minventory_resupply_form.xml.

We then define <MODULE_DIR>/Block/Adminhtml/Product/Edit/Button/Back.php as follows:

```
class Back extends \Magento\Backend\Block\Template implements
\Magento\Framework\View\Element\UiComponent\Control\ButtonProviderInterface
{
  public function getButtonData() {
    return [
      'label' => __('Back'),
      'on_click' => sprintf("location.href = '%s';", $this->getBackUrl()),
      'class' => 'back',
      'sort_order' => 10
    ];
  }

  public function getBackUrl() {
```

```
        return $this->getUrl('*/*/');
    }
}
```

The `ButtonProviderInterface` requires the `getButtonData` method implementation. The structure of the return array is somewhat blurry until we gloss over some of the other buttons that are defined across Magento. This renders our **Back** button as follows:

```
<button id="back" title="Back" type="button" class="action- scalable back"
onclick="location.href = '... stripped away ...';" data-ui-id="back-
button">
    <span>Back</span>
</button>
```

The **Back** button provides a *go back to previous page* functionality, which in our case is determined by the value of the `getBackUrl` method response.

We then define `<MODULE_DIR>/Block/Adminhtml/Product/Edit/Button/Save.php` as follows:

```
class Save extends \Magento\Backend\Block\Template implements
\Magento\Framework\View\Element\UiComponent\Control\ButtonProviderInterface
{
  public function getButtonData() {
    return [
      'label' => __('Save'),
      'class' => 'save primary',
      'data_attribute' => [
        'mage-init' => ['button' => ['event' => 'save']],
        'form-role' => 'save',
      ],
      'sort_order' => 20,
    ];
  }
}
```

Much like with the previous button, we use a similar array structure for our button here. The difference is that this time we are passing the `data_attribute` as well. This renders our **Save** button as follows:

```
<button id="save" title="Save" type="button" class="action- scalable save
primary ui-button ui-widget ui-state-default ui-corner-all ui-button-text-
only" onclick="location.href = '... stripped away ...';" data-form-
role="save" data-ui-id="save-button" role="button" aria-
disabled="false"><span class="ui-button-text">
    <span>Save</span>
</span></button>
```

The `mage-init` part might seem confusing at the moment. Suffice it to say that it's a way of initializing a JS component, which is something we will address in more detail in the next chapter. Our **Save** essentially triggers the form's submission.

With this we have finished our `form` component definition, making the whole **Stock Resupply** screen functional.

Summary

In this chapter, we built two very different screens in the Magento admin area. One utilized the `listing` component, whereas the other utilized the `form` component. A great deal of our work involved configuration rather than coding, which stands to prove how powerful Magento UI components can be. While the amount of configuration might seem overwhelming at first, getting a grip on individual component configurations allows us to build complex interfaces quickly.

Moving forward, we are going to take a look at some of the specifics behind developing for the storefront area.

6
Developing for Storefront

The Magento *storefront* is the customer-facing view of a Magento e-commerce platform. Developing for *storefront* implies developing for the frontend area. Whereas the `adminhtml` area is primarily built via means of UI components, the frontend area makes heavy use of **JavaScript (JS)** components that come in form of *jQuery widgets* and *UI/KnockoutJS components*. Aside from JS components, there are lots of other bits and pieces involved in storefront development, such as themes, layouts, templates, language packages, and CSS/LESS. Our focus, however, throughout this chapter will be on JS components, as they seem to be the most confusing and challenging part of the Magento frontend to overcome.

Moving forward, we are going to look into the following sections:

- Setting up the playground
- Initializing JS components
- Meet RequireJS
- Replacing jQuery widget components
- Extending jQuery widgets components
- Creating jQuery widgets components
- Extending UI/KnockoutJS components
- Creating UI/KnockoutJS components

Technical requirements

You will need to have basic knowledge of PHP, OOP, JavaScript, and XML. You will also need Apache, MySQL, and AMPPS installed on your system to execute the codes.

The code files of this chapter can be found on GitHub: `https://github.com/PacktPublishing/Magento-2-Quick-Start-Guide`.

Check out the following video to see the Code in Action:

`http://bit.ly/2D6oMLz`.

Setting up the playground

To get a better understanding of the `frontend` area, we are going to build a very lightweight `Magelicious_Jsco` module, to serve as a playground for our JS component exploration.

To this point, we should already be pretty familiar with the flow of creating a new module. Assuming we have defined our basic `registration.php`, `composer.json`, and `etc/module.xml` files, we can start dealing with the specifics of our `Magelicious_Jsco` module.

Let's start by defining `<MODULE_DIR>/etc/frontend/routes.xml`, as follows:

```
<config>
    <router id="standard">
        <route id="jsco" frontName="jsco">
            <module name="Magelicious_Jsco"/>
        </route>
    </router>
</config>
```

We then create `<MODULE_DIR>/Controller/Playground.php`, as follows:

```
namespace Magelicious\Jsco\Controller;
abstract class Playground extends \Magento\Framework\App\Action\Action
{
}
```

We then create `<MODULE_DIR>/Controller/Playground/Index.php`, as follows:

```
namespace Magelicious\Jsco\Controller\Playground;
use Magento\Framework\Controller\ResultFactory;
class Index extends \Magelicious\Jsco\Controller\Playground
{
    public function execute() {
        $resultPage =
$this->resultFactory->create(ResultFactory::TYPE_PAGE);
        $resultPage->getConfig()->getTitle()->set(__('Playground'));
        return $resultPage;
    }
}
```

There's nothing really new to this point. We have merely created a route, controller, and controller action to support a *page* that we can access via the URL, such as `http://magelicious.loc/jsco/playground`. But the page itself is defined via XML layout, and we further create `<MODULE_DIR>/view/frontend/layout/jsco_playground_index.xml`, as follows:

```
<page xmlns:xsi="http://www.w3.org/2001/XMLSchema-instance" layout="empty"
xsi:noNamespaceSchemaLocation="urn:magento:framework:View/Layout/etc/page_c
onfiguration.xsd">
  <body>
    <referenceContainer name="content">
      <block class="Magelicious\Jsco\Block\Test"
            name="jsco_test"
            template="Magelicious_Jsco::playground.phtml">
      </block>
    </referenceContainer>
  </body>
</page>
```

Note `layout="empty"` he

re; this is to limit ourselves to a nearly empty page to work with.

Finally, we create an empty `<MODULE_DIR>view/frontend/templates/playground.phtml` page. If we were to now open a link, such as `http://magelicious.loc/jsco/playground`, that would open a page with the **Playground** title shown. `playground.phtml` is where all of our sample code will go in, as we continue exploring this chapter.

Calling and initializing JS components

Calling and initializing JS components might seem a bit challenging at first. There are two types of syntax notations used with Magento JS components:

- **Declarative:**
  - Using the `data-mage-init` attribute
  - Using the `<script type="text/x-magento-init" />` tag
- **Imperative:**
  - Using the `<script>` tag, without the `type="text/x-magento-init"` attribute

To better understand the `data-mage-init` notation, let's take a look at a partial `<PROJECT_DIR>/lib/web/mage/redirect-url.js` file extract:

```
define([
    'jquery',
    'jquery/ui'
], function ($) {
    'use strict';
    $.widget('mage.redirectUrl', {
        options: {
            event: 'click',
            url: undefined
        },
        _bind: function () { /* ... */ },
        _create: function () { /* ... */ },
        _onEvent: function () { /* ... */ }
    });
    return $.mage.redirectUrl;
});
```

This here is a jQuery widget wrapped as an *AMD module*; more on that later on. `data-mage-init` knows how to interpret `mage.redirectUrl` as a `redirectUrl` component. By studying the `redirectUrl` widget code, we can see it can be used not only with the button and the link type of elements but with the `select` type as well. Let's go ahead and append our `playground.phtml` file with the following:

```
<a data-mage-init='{"redirectUrl":{"url":"http://test.url"}}'>
    <span><?= __('Test') ?></span>
</a>

<button type="button"
        data-mage-init='{"redirectUrl":{"url":"http://test.url"}}'>
```

```
    <span><?= __('Test') ?></span>
</button>

<select data-mage-init='{"redirectUrl": {"event":"change"}}'>
    <option value="http://test.url/1">Test#1</option>
    <option value="http://test.url/2">Test#2</option>
    <option value="http://test.url/3">Test#3</option>
</select>
```

While the `click` event works perfectly for link and button elements, the `select` element relies on a more specific `change` event. Therefore, our `select` element exploits the fact that the `redirectUrl` component accepts the event configuration option. This makes for a nice and clean little example of reusing a single component multiple time.

To better understand the `<script type="text/x-magento-init" />` notation, let's take a look at a partial `<MAGENTO_DIR>/module-cookie/view/frontend/web/js/notices.js` file extract:

```
define([
    'jquery',
    'jquery/ui',
    'mage/cookies'
], function ($) {
    'use strict';
    $.widget('mage.cookieNotices', {
        _create: function () {
            //...
        }
    });
    return $.mage.cookieNotices;
});
```

Just like in our first example, this is just another jQuery widget essentially. What the `cookieNotices` widget does is take the given content and display it as cookie notice alert to the user, doing so until the user finally hits the **Allow Cookies** button. We can easily reuse this widget to inject our own content. While both `cookieNotices` and `redirectUrl` are jQuery widgets, the way they are used in Magento differs.

Let's go ahead and append our `playground.phtml` file with the following HTML bits:

```
<div id="playgroundCookieBlock" class="message global cookie"
style="display: none;">
  <p>
    <strong><?= $block->escapeHtml(__('We use cookies to make your
experience better.')) ?></strong>
    <span><?= $block->escapeHtml(__('To comply with the new e-Privacy
```

```
directive, we need to ask for your consent to set the cookies.')) ?></span>
    <?= $block->escapeHtml(__('<a href="%1">Learn more</a>.',
'http://magelicious.loc/privacy'), ['a']) ?>
  </p>
  <div class="actions">
    <button id="btn-cookie-allow" class="action allow primary">
      <span><?= $block->escapeHtml(__('Allow Cookies')) ?></span>
    </button>
  </div>
</div>
```

This is to simulate our intent for a custom cookie widget, with special content and a cookie name. Let's further append the `playground.phtml` file with a declarative call to `cookieNotices` JS component:

```
<script type="text/x-magento-init">
  {
    "#playgroundCookieBlock": {
      "cookieNotices": {
        "cookieAllowButtonSelector": "#btn-cookie-allow",
        "cookieName": "playgroundCookie",
        "cookieValue": "playgroundCookieValue",
        "cookieLifetime": "300",
        "noCookiesUrl": "http://magelicious.loc/no-cookies"
      }
    }
  }
</script>
```

Unlike the `redirectUrl` widget, which had a nice list of `options` defined at the very start of the widget definition, the `cookieNotices` widget does not have those. It merely references those options throughout the code, via `this.options.<optionPushedViaMagentoInit>` calls. This is really a default jQuery widget `options` object. The reason we are bringing it up is merely to understand how, most of the time, one needs to take a more involved approach toward inspecting existing JavaScript components code, instead of just focusing on the set of possible default options.

To better understand the `<script>` tag notation, let's take a look at a partial `<MAGENTO_DIR>/module-ui/view/base/web/js/modal/modal.js` file extract:

```
define([
  /* ... */
], function ( /* ... */ ) {
  'use strict';
  //...
  $.widget('mage.modal', {
```

```
    //...
  });
  return $.mage.modal;
});
```

As in the previous two examples, this again is just a jQuery widget. Now let's go ahead and append our `playground.phtml` file with the following HTML bits:

```
<div>
  <a href="#" id="playgroundModalLink">Show modal!</a>
</div>

<div id="playgroundModal">
  <p>Content...</p>
</div>
```

This is to simulate our intent of creating a modal box, with special content. Now, let's use the `modal` widget to turn this into an actual modal. We further append our `playground.phtml` file, as follows:

```
<script>
  require([
      'jquery',
      'mage/translate',
      'Magento_Ui/js/modal/modal'
    ], function ($, $t, modal) {
      var options = {
        title: 'Playground Modal',
        buttons: [{
          text: $t('Continue'),
          click: function () {
            this.closeModal();
          }
        }]
      };

      modal(options, $('#playgroundModal'));

      $('#playgroundModalLink').on('click', function () {
        $('#playgroundModal').modal('openModal');
      });
    }
  );
</script>
```

This time we are using the `<script>` tag approach to utilize the JS component.

To ensure our code evaluates on page load, we can further wrap our `modal` widget related code into a function, as follows:

```
<script>
  require([
      /* libraries ... */
    ], function ( /* params ... */ ) {
      $(function () {
        // Raw JS code...
      });
    }
  );
</script>
```

Likewise, we can use a RequireJS `domReady` module to execute our JS code on DOM:

```
<script>
  require([
    'jquery',
    'mage/translate',
    'domReady!'
  ], function ($, $t) {
    // Raw JS code...
  });
</script>
```

The `!` character used in `domReady!` is a syntax reserved for plugins. While there is more to it, suffice to say that in a case of `domReady!` the plugin exists simply as a way of waiting until DOM gets loaded before invoking our function.

The choice of calling and initializing JS components depends on how they are written and how they are intended to be used. We use the *declarative* notation when our component requires initialization. The configuration is prepared on the backend and simply outputted to the page. We use the *imperative* notation on the pages that use raw JS code; this allows us to execute particular business logic.

Meet RequireJS

To this point, we have been using things like `redirectUrl` and `cookieNotices` out of thin air, but how exactly do these components become available to our code? The answer is, via RequireJS, a library that underlies nearly every other JS feature built into Magento. The overall role of RequireJS is simple; it is a JS module system that implements the **Asynchronous Module Definition (AMD)** standard, which serves as an improvement over the web's current `globals` and `script` tags.

We have already seen the format of these AMD modules in the preceding examples, which comes down the following:

```
define(['dep1', 'dep2'], function (dep1, dep2) {
  return function () {
    // Module value to return
  };
});
```

The gist of AMD modules functionality comes down to each module being able to:

- Register the factory function via `define`
- Inject dependencies, instead of using globals
- Execute the factory function when all dependencies become accessible
- Pass dependent modules as arguments to the factory function

This strategy solves many of the conventional dependency issues, where dependencies are assumed to be immediately available when the function executes, which is not always the case.

If we were to do a **View Page Source** on our **Playground** page in a browser, we would see three `<script type="text/javascript" src="...">` tags with their `src` attributes pointing to the following JS files:

```
frontend/Magento/luma/en_US/requirejs/require.js
frontend/Magento/luma/en_US/mage/requirejs/mixins.js
frontend/Magento/luma/en_US/requirejs-config.js
```

A quick look at the partial `requirejs-config.js` file reveals how these get loaded:

```
(function (require) {
  /* ... */
  (function () {
    var config = {
      map: {
        '*': {
```

```
            'redirectUrl': 'mage/redirect-url',
        }
    }
};
require.config(config);
})();
/* ... */
(function () {
    var config = {
        map: {
            '*': {
                cookieNotices: 'Magento_Cookie/js/notices'
            }
        }
    };
    require.config(config);
})();
/* ... */
})(require);
```

These two mappings break down as follows:

- The *left-hand side* points to the freely given name of our JS component, which essentially tells consumers how to reference it. This is why we were able to use these two components simply by referencing them via `redirectUrl` and `cookieNotices`.

- The *right-hand side* points to the location of our JS component:
    - `mage/redirect-url`, where `mage` points to the `<PROJECT_DIR>/lib/web/mage` directory, and `redirect-url` further points to the `redirect-url.js` file within that directory
    - `Magento_Cookie/js/notices`, where `Magento_Cookie` points to the `<MAGENTO_DIR>/module-cookie/view/frontend/web` directory, and `js/notices` further points to the `js/notices.js` file within that directory

Further observing the `requirejs-config.js` file, aside from `map`, there are a few other important keys whose roles are worth knowing:

```
var config = {
    map: {
        '*': {
            /* ... */
        }
```

```
    },
    paths: {
        /* ... */
    },
    shim: {
        /* ... */
    },
    deps: [
        /* ... */
    ],
    config: {
        mixins: {
            /* ... */
        }
    }
};
```

These break down as follows:

- `map`: For the given module prefix; instead of loading the module with the given ID, substitute a different module ID
- `paths`: Path mappings for module names not found directly under `baseUrl`
- `shim`: Configure the dependencies, exports, and custom initialization for older *browser globals* scripts that do not use `define` for declaring the dependencies and setting the module value
- `deps`: An array of dependencies to load
- `config`/`mixins`: List of JS class mappings, for classes whose methods are added to, or mixed in, with other JS classes

 See `https://requirejs.org/docs/api.html` for more information on the RequireJS API.

The takeaway here is that our own modules can define the `requirejs-config.js` file on their own, under the `<MODULE_DIR>/view/frontend` directory, allowing us to hook into the final Magento `requirejs-config.js` file that gets generated for the browser. This, in turn, allows us to easily register our own components, override existing mappings, paths, and other things.

Replacing jQuery widget components

While the majority of the time, we would want to leave the existing JS components to work their magic as is, there are times when business requirements are drastic enough to make the whole component unusable. Thinking in terms of PHP classes, we can imagine that class *A implements X*, whereas we want to have a completely different implementation of *X*, let's call it *B*, that shares very little with *A*. This is a case where simply having *B extends A* would not suffice, so we opt for directly *B implements X*. While there are no interfaces in pure JS, this does not mean we cannot completely replace one concrete class with another, as long as we ensure those few crucial methods are available via the new class.

Replacing JS classes is easy with Magento. Let's imagine we want to fully replace the `redirectUrl` component.

We start by creating the `<MODULE_DIR>/view/frontend/requirejs-config.js` file, as follows:

```
var config = {
  map: {
    '*': {
      redirectUrl: 'Magelicious_Jsco/js/redirect-url'
    }
  }
};
```

We then implement the actual `Magelicious_Jsco/js/redirect-url` as part of the `<MODULE_DIR>/view/frontend/web/js/redirect-url.js` file, as follows.

```
define([
    'jquery',
], function ($) {
    'use strict';
    $.widget('magelicious.redirectUrl', {
        _create: function () {
            // New implementation
            console.log('magelicious.redirectUrl');
        }
    });
    return $.magelicious.redirectUrl;
});
```

`magelicious.redirectUrl` matches the new name of our widget, whereas `magelicious` is our *namespace* and `redirectUrl` is the actual *name of the widget* within our namespace.

Once we refresh the static content via the `php bin/magento setup:static-content:deploy` command, we should now be able to see `magelicious.redirectUrl` show up in the browser console window. Clearly, the current implementation of `redirectUrl` would break the functionality we had with the original component, but it goes to show how easily we can fully replace the component with a new one.

Extending jQuery widget components

Assuming we wish to extend the `redirectUrl` component instead of replacing it completely, we can do so in a similar fashion. The entry in our `requirejs-config.js` remains the same, whereas the difference lies in how we edit our `redirect-url.js` file:

```
define([
  'jquery',
  'jquery/ui',
  'mage/redirect-url'
], function ($) {
  'use strict';
  $.widget('magelicious.redirectUrl', $.mage.redirectUrl, {
  /* Override of parent _onEvent method */
  _onEvent: function () {
  // Call parent's _onEvent() method if needed
  return this._super();
  }
  });
  return $.magelicious.redirectUrl;
});
```

Using the `_super` or `_superApply` is a jQuery widget way of invoking methods of the same name in the parent widget. While this approach works, there is a more elegant solution called **mixins**.

The Magento mixins for JS are much like its plugins for PHP. To convert to the *mixin* approach, we replace our `requirejs-config.js` with content, as follows.

```
var config = {
  config: {
    mixins: {
      'mage/redirect-url': {
        'Magelicious_Jsco/js/redirect-url-mixin': true
      }
    }
  }
};
```

Note, that this time we are using the full path `'mage/redirect-url'` instead of the `redirectUrl` alias on the left side of the mapping, whereas the right side of mapping points to our *mixin*. The convention is to use the `-mixing` suffix on top of the original JS filename.

We then create `<MODULE_DIR>/view/frontend/web/js/redirect-url-mixin.js` with content, as follows:

```
define([
 'jquery'
], function ($) {
 return function (originalWidget) {
 $.widget(
 'magelicious.redirectUrl',
 originalWidget, {
 /* Redefined _onEvent method */
 _onEvent: function () {
 console.log('_onEvent via mixin');
 // Call parent's _onEvent() method if needed
 return this._super();
 }
 }
 );
 return $.magelicious.redirectUrl;
 };
});
```

The example here might not do justice, as it merely looks more complex than the previous example of directly extending the widget. This is because we cannot simply do `originalWidget._onEvent = function () { /* ... */ };` or `originalWidget._proto._onEvent = function () { /* ... */ };` and thus override the widget method. Widget methods need to be overridden on the prototype, which, in our case, essentially means creating a new widget from the original.

If we were adding a mixin for a non-widget type of JS, such as
`Magento_Checkout/js/action/place-order`, then the approach would be different, as
shown in `Magento_CheckoutAgreements/js/model/place-order-mixin`.

Creating jQuery widgets components

Creating simple jQuery widgets components is pretty straightforward from a Magento
point of view. The actual knowledge of building robust jQuery widgets depends on our
knowledge of jQuery itself.

Let's assume our widget will be called `welcome`, and its purpose is to simply output
Welcome %name% to the element, provided we passed on the `name` option during widget
initialization.

We start by adding the mapping under our `<MODULE_DIR>/view/frontend/requirejs-config.js` file, as follows:

```
var config = {
  map: {
    '*': {
      welcome: 'Magelicious_Jsco/js/welcome'
    }
  }
};
```

We then define the widget itself, as part of the
`<MODULE_DIR>/view/frontend/web/js/welcome.js` file, as follows:

```
define([
  'jquery',
  'mage/translate'
], function ($, $t) {
  'use strict';
  $.widget('magelicious.welcome', {
    _create: function () {
      this.element.text($t('Welcome ' + this.options.name));
    }
  });
  return $.magelicious.welcome;
});
```

We can see that our widget is quite simple. If we now run Magento's `setup:static-content:deploy` command, our widget should already be ready for use, as we can now initialize it from template files.

Finally, let's initialize our welcome widget by amending `playground.phtml`, as follows:

```php
<?php $helper = $this->helper('Magento\Framework\Json\Helper\Data') ?>

<span data-mage-init='<?= $helper->jsonEncode(
    ['welcome' => ['name' => 'John Doe']]
) ?>'></span>
```

With this in place, we should now be able to see the **Welcome John Doe** message in our browser. While this little component seems quite an overkill for what it does, the concepts behind it are what matters.

 See `https://api.jqueryui.com/jquery.widget/` for more information on creating jQuery widgets.

Creating UI/KnockoutJS components

To this point, we have only been dealing with jQuery widgets as components. While extremely powerful, jQuery widgets are not best suited for rendering robust components with complex HTML structures. The other type of JS components is what we refer to as UI/KnockoutJS components. Built on the shoulders of the KnockoutJS library, these components allow powerful templating of our data, among other things. Without getting too deep into the ins and outs of these type of components, suffice to say that the main construct we are referring to when we speak of UI/KnockoutJS components is `uiComponent`.

As per `<MAGENTO_DIR>/module-ui/view/base/requirejs-config.js`, the `uiComponent` maps to the `Magento_Ui/js/lib/core/collection` JS file. Inspecting the `collection.js` file, we can see that `uiComponent` extends `uiElement`, which maps to the `Magento_Ui/js/lib/core/element/element` JS file. The `uiComponent` and `uiElement` make use of the `ko`, `underscore`, `mageUtils`, `uiRegistry`, `uiEvents`, and `uiClass` libraries, among other things, so it's worth getting ourselves familiar with those.

Creating new UI/KnockoutJS components is a slightly more involved process than creating a jQuery widget.

We start by creating the proper mapping under our `<MODULE_DIR>/view/frontend/requirejs-config.js` file, as follows:

```
var config = {
  map: {
    '*': {
      popularProducts: 'Magelicious_Jsco/js/popular-products'
    }
  }
};
```

This part is the same as with jQuery widgets. Here we simply register, or alias if you will, our component name to its file location.

We then define the component itself, under the `<MODULE_DIR>/view/frontend/web/js/popular-products.js` file, as follows:

```
define([
    'jquery',
    'uiComponent',
    'ko',
    'mage/translate'
], function ($, Component, ko, $t) {
    'use strict';
    return Component.extend({
      defaults: {
        template: 'Magelicious_Jsco/popular-products',
        title: $t('Popular Products'),
        products: [],
      },
      getTitle: function () {
        return this.title;
      }
    });
  }
);
```

The basis of all UI components is `uiComponent`. We pass on the instance of `uiComponent` as a `Component` parameter. We then implement the specifics of our component as part of the JSON object passed onto the `Component.extend` method.

With our component JS file now in place, we further create the template file referenced by the component. We do so under the `<MODULE_DIR>/view/frontend/web/template/popular-products.html` file, as follows:

```html
<h4 data-bind="text: getTitle()"></h4>
<ul data-bind="foreach: products">
  <li>
    <span>
      <span data-bind="text: title"></span>
      (<span data-bind="text: sku"></span>)
    </span>
  </li>
</ul>
```

What happens in the HTML template files is all about KnockoutJS, which means a certain part of the KnockoutJS library is required in order to built UI/KnockoutJS components.

See `http://knockoutjs.com` for more information on the KnockoutJS library.

We then amend our `jsco_playground_index.xml` by adding the following line under `<referenceContainer name="content">`:

```xml
<block name="popular_products"
  template="Magelicious_Jsco::popular-products.phtml" />
```

`popular-products.phtml` is where we will instantiate our UI/KnockoutJS component.

Finally, we create `<MODULE_DIR>/view/frontend/templates/popular-products.phtml` with content, as follows:

```php
<?php $jsonHelper = $this->helper('Magento\Framework\Json\Helper\Data'); ?>

<div class="popular-products" data-bind="scope:'popular-products-scope'">
  <!-- ko template: getTemplate() --><!-- /ko -->
</div>

<script type="text/x-magento-init">
  {
    ".popular-products": {
      "Magento_Ui/js/core/app": {
        "components": {
          "popular-products-scope": {
```

```
            "component": "popularProducts",
            "products": <?= /* @escapeNotVerified */
$jsonHelper->jsonEncode([
                ['sku' => 'sku1', 'title' => 'Title1'],
                ['sku' => 'sku2', 'title' => 'Title2']
            ]) ?>
        }
      }
    }
  }
}
</script>
```

Here we are using the declarative approach to initialize our component. The structure of the JSON object under the `script` tag might seem a bit confusing at first. The `.popular-products` key is essentially a selector, targeting whatever HTML element it might find. `Magento_Ui/js/core/app` is an alias for the `app.js` file, which creates the UI components instances according to the configuration of the JSON using the `uiLayout` component. `components` is a key under which we nest one or more components we wish to initialize. `popular-products-scope` is sort of a scope key assigned to our component, which we use to `data-bind` the `scope` value to the HTML element.

Clearing the cache and redeploying the static files, we should now be able to see our newly created component.

Extending UI/KnockoutJS components

Extending UI/KnockoutJS components is a process similar to extending the jQuery widgets. Let's for a moment assume we have the `Magelicious_Jsco2` module that wants to override our `popularProducts` component.

The way to do it would be to add the proper mapping under the map key of our `<MODULE2_DIR>/view/frontend/requirejs-config.js` file:

```
var config = {
  map: {
    '*': {
      popularProducts: 'Magelicious_Jsco2/js/new-popular-products'
    }
  }
};
```

We then create the proper `new-popular-products.js` file, as follows:

```
define([
    'jquery',
    'Magelicious_Jsco/js/popular-products',
    'ko',
    'mage/translate',
], function ($, popularProductsComponent, ko, $t) {
    'use strict';
    return popularProductsComponent.extend({
      getTitle: function () {
        return 'NEW | ' + this._super();
      }
    });
  }
);
```

The example here shows that we are no longer passing in the instance of `uiComponent`, rather the instance of the original `Magelicious_Jsco/js/popular-products` that we wish to extend. Simply using the `extend` method on our `popularProductsComponent` object allows us to extend it easily. By redefining the methods of the same name, such as `getTitle`, we effectively override the same method on the component we are running the `extend` on.

Summary

Though there are lots of other bits and pieces involved in storefront development, JS components make for the most challenging part of it. Understanding how to write new components, as well as how to override or bypass existing ones is an essential skill for any Magento developer, be it backend or frontend. Admittedly, this chapter took more of a *backend/module-developer* type of an approach on the subject.

Whenever there is a need to change the behavior of the underlying component, whether it is pure JS, a jQuery widget, or UI/KnockoutJS, we should consider the scope of changes in order to decide whether we should approach it by *replacing*, *overriding*, or using *mixin*.

Moving forward, we are going to take a look at some of the neat things we can do around customizing the storefront catalog behavior, most of which come down to *plugins* and *JS components*.

7
Customizing Catalog Behavior

Right out of the box, Magento provides a pretty robust catalog functionality. Managing categories and products on a *multi-store*, *multi-currency*, *multi-language* level with a support for custom attributes, catalog search, catalog rules, and alike are features that are likely to suffice for most customers. Sometimes, however, certain integrations or larger and smaller features are requested, that build on top of the existing functionality. Whether to improve user experience or accommodate essential business requirements, catalog customization's play a major role in everyday Magento development.

We are going to customize our catalog behavior by:

- Creating the size guide
- Creating the same day delivery
- Flagging new products

These stand only as a small fragment of what's possible with Magento catalog customizations.

Moving forward, our work is to be done as part of the `Magelicious_Catalog` module, which we will develop throughout the chapter.

Technical requirements

You will need to have basic knowledge of PHP, OOP, JavaScript, and XML. You will also need Apache, MySQL, and AMPPS installed on your system to execute the codes.

The code files of this chapter can be found on GitHub:
`https://github.com/PacktPublishing/Magento-2-Quick-Start-Guide`.

Check out the following video to see the Code in Action:

`http://bit.ly/2MFJaCN`.

Creating the size guide

We have been asked to add a functionality that shows the *size guide* on a *product view* page. This is to appear as a new tab next to the existing **Details**, **More Information**, and **Reviews** tabs. The content of the *size guide* tab is to be the same for all products containing the `size` attribute. We also need it to be editable from Magento admin.

Let's take a moment to think about our approach here:

- To be the same for all products and editable from *Magento admin* needs the CMS block
- The *CMS block* needs *setup script* for creating the size guide block
- To **Appear as a new tab** next to the existing tabs requires a `catalog_product_view.xml` layout update

Assuming we have defined `registration.php`, `composer.json`, and `etc/module.xml` as basic module files, we can deal with the more specific details of our `Magelicious_Catalog` module.

We start by defining <MODULE_DIR>/Setup/InstallData.php with content, as follows:

```
namespace Magelicious\Catalog\Setup;
class InstallData implements \Magento\Framework\Setup\InstallDataInterface
{
  protected $searchCriteriaBuilder;
  protected $blockRepository;
  protected $blockFactory;

  public function __construct(
    \Magento\Framework\Api\SearchCriteriaBuilder $searchCriteriaBuilder,
    \Magento\Cms\Api\BlockRepositoryInterface $blockRepository,
    \Magento\Cms\Api\Data\BlockInterfaceFactory $blockFactory
  ) {
    $this->searchCriteriaBuilder = $searchCriteriaBuilder;
    $this->blockRepository = $blockRepository;
    $this->blockFactory = $blockFactory;
  }

  public function install(
    \Magento\Framework\Setup\ModuleDataSetupInterface $setup,
    \Magento\Framework\Setup\ModuleContextInterface $context
  ) {
    $setup->startSetup();
    $searchCriteria = $this->searchCriteriaBuilder
      ->addFilter('identifier', 'size-guide', 'eq')
```

```
    ->create();
  $blocks = $this->blockRepository->getList($searchCriteria)->getItems();
  if (empty($blocks)) {
    /* @var \Magento\Cms\Api\Data\BlockInterface $block */
    $block = $this->blockFactory->create();
    $block->setIdentifier('size-guide');
    $block->setTitle('Size Guide');
    $block->setContent('Size guide!');
    $this->blockRepository->save($block);
  }
  $setup->endSetup();
  }
}
```

The InstallData script ensures that the size-guide CMS block is created during module installation if it does not already exist. With this in place, we can already run the setup:upgrade command. This should install our module and create the size-guide CMS block.

We then define <MODULE_DIR>/Block/SizeGuide.php with content, as follows:

```
namespace Magelicious\Catalog\Block;
class SizeGuide extends \Magento\Cms\Block\Block implements
\Magento\Framework\DataObject\IdentityInterface {
  protected $product;
  protected $coreRegistry;

  public function __construct(
    \Magento\Framework\View\Element\Context $context,
    \Magento\Cms\Model\Template\FilterProvider $filterProvider,
    \Magento\Store\Model\StoreManagerInterface $storeManager,
    \Magento\Cms\Model\BlockFactory $blockFactory,
    \Magento\Framework\Registry $coreRegistry,
    array $data = []
  ) {
    $this->coreRegistry = $coreRegistry;
    parent::__construct($context, $filterProvider, $storeManager,
$blockFactory, $data);
  }
  public function _toHtml() { /* ... */ }
  public function getProduct() {
    if (!$this->product) {
      $this->product = $this->coreRegistry->registry('product');
    }
    return $this->product;
  }
}
```

This is the actual block class that we will output on the *product view* page. The registry's object `product` key is already set by the parent class up the layout tree. This allows us to easily fetch the instance of the current product.

The `_toHtml` method is further implemented, as follows:

```
protected function _toHtml()
{
  if ($this->getProduct()->getTypeId() ==
\Magento\ConfigurableProduct\Model\Product\Type\Configurable::TYPE_CODE) {
    $configurableAttributes =
$this->getProduct()->getTypeInstance()->getConfigurableAttributesAsArray($t
his->getProduct());
    foreach ($configurableAttributes as $attribute) {
      if (isset($attribute['attribute_code']) &&
$attribute['attribute_code'] == 'size') {
        return parent::_toHtml();
      }
    }
  }
  return '';
}
```

This is the gist of our *size guide* functionality. The *configurable type* and *size attribute code* checks ensure that the output of `_toHtml` renders the `size-guide` block only for certain groups of products.

We finally define
`<MODULE_DIR>/view/frontend/layout/catalog_product_view.xml` with content, as follows:

```
<page>
  <body>
    <referenceBlock name="product.info.details">
      <block class="Magelicious\Catalog\Block\SizeGuide" name="size-guide"
after="-" group="detailed_info">
        <arguments>
          <argument name="block_id" xsi:type="string">size-guide</argument>
          <argument name="css_class"
xsi:type="string">description</argument>
          <argument name="at_label" xsi:type="string">none</argument>
          <argument name="title" translate="true" xsi:type="string">Size
Guide</argument>
        </arguments>
      </block>
```

```
    </referenceBlock>
  </body>
</page>
```

This is the glue that binds our `SizeGuide` block to a *product view* page, and, more specifically, the `product.info.details` block that neatly contains the **Details**, **More Information**, and **Reviews** tabs.

The final *product view* page result should look like this:

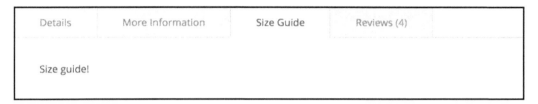

Creating the same day delivery

We have been asked to add a functionality that shows an *active countdown* with a **You have %h %min %sec to catch our same day delivery offer** message on a *product view* page, whereas the countdown is based on an *optionally* assigned daily `cutoffAt` time, set for every product individually, for every day of a week independently.

Let's take a moment to think about our approach here:

- *Every product* and *every day of a week* imply Monday to Sunday _[Cutoff_At] product attributes
- Product attributes imply setup script
- *Active countdown* implies JS components

We start by bumping up the `setup_version` value of our `<MODULE_DIR>/etc/module.xml` file from `1.0.0` to `1.0.1`. This allows us to introduce the `<MODULE_DIR>/Setup/UpgradeData.php` file with an upgrade, as follows:

```
protected function upgradeToVersionOneZeroOne(
  \Magento\Framework\Setup\ModuleDataSetupInterface $setup
) {
  $eavSetup = $this->eavSetupFactory->create(['setup' => $setup]);

  $days = [
    'monday', 'tuesday', 'wednesday', 'thursday',
```

```
    'friday', 'saturday', 'sunday'
];

$sortOrder = 100;

foreach ($days as $day) {
  $eavSetup->addAttribute(
    \Magento\Catalog\Model\Product::ENTITY,
    $day . '_cutoff_at',
    [
      'type' => 'varchar',
      'label' => ucfirst($day) . ' Cutoff At',
      'input' => 'text',
      'required' => false,
      'sort_order' => $sortOrder++,
      'global' =>
\Magento\Eav\Model\Entity\Attribute\ScopedAttributeInterface::SCOPE_STORE,
      'group' => 'Cutoff',
    ]
  );
  }
}
```

The addAttribute method here is run for each day of the week, thus creating monday_cutoff_at to sunday_cutoff_at product attributes. If, at this point, we were to run the Magento's setup:upgrade command, our UpgradeData script would get executed and schema_version and data_version numbers from within the setup_module table would get bumped to the 1.0.1 version. Likewise, going into the Magento admin area and *editing* or *creating a new* product, would show the following screen. This is where we enable the user to enter the time of the day in an <hour>:<minute> format, such as **15:30**. This time, if entered, will later be used by the JS component to render the countdown functionality on the storefront product view page:

Cutoff

Monday Cutoff At [store view]	
Tuesday Cutoff At [store view]	
Wednesday Cutoff At [store view]	
Thursday Cutoff At [store view]	
Friday Cutoff At [store view]	
Saturday Cutoff At [store view]	
Sunday Cutoff At [store view]	

We then create `<MODULE_DIR>/Block/Product/View/Cutoff.php`, as follows:

```php
namespace Magelicious\Catalog\Block\Product\View;

class Cutoff extends \Magento\Framework\View\Element\Template implements
\Magento\Framework\DataObject\IdentityInterface
{
    private $product;
    protected $coreRegistry;
    protected $localeDate;

    public function __construct(
        \Magento\Framework\View\Element\Template\Context $context,
        \Magento\Framework\Registry $coreRegistry,
        \Magento\Framework\Stdlib\DateTime\TimezoneInterface $localeDate,
        array $data = []
    ) {
        $this->coreRegistry = $coreRegistry;
        $this->localeDate = $localeDate;
        parent::__construct($context, $data);
    }

    public function getProduct() { /* ... */ }
```

```
        public function getCutoffAt() { /* ... */ }
        public function getIdentities() { /* ... */ }
    }
```

We will use this class when we reach our layout update.

The getProduct method is further implemented, as follows:

```
    public function getProduct()
    {
      if (!$this->product) {
        $this->product = $this->coreRegistry->registry('product');
      }
      return $this->product;
    }
```

As mentioned previously, the registry's product key is already set by the parent class up the layout tree, so we exploit that fact to fetch the current product.

The getCutoffAt method is further implemented, as follows:

```
    public function getCutoffAt()
    {
      $timezone = new \DateTimeZone($this->localeDate->getConfigTimezone());
      $now = new \DateTime('now', $timezone);
      $day = strtolower($now->format('l'));
      $cutoffAt = $this->getProduct()->getData($day . '_cutoff_at');
      if ($cutoffAt) {
        $timeForDay = \DateTime::createFromFormat(
          'Y-m-d H:i',
          $now->format('Y-m-d') . ' ' . $cutoffAt,
          $timezone
        );

        if ($timeForDay instanceof \DateTime) {
          return $timeForDay->format(DATE_ISO8601);
        }
      }
      return 0;
    }
```

This is the gist of our *same day delivery* functionality from the PHP side of things. We ensure we properly return the full date and time based on the product's $day . '_cutoff_at' attribute value; this will later be passed onto the JS component.

Finally, the getIdentities method is further implemented, as follows:

```
public function getIdentities()
{
  $identities = $this->getProduct()->getIdentities();
  $timezone = new \DateTimeZone($this->localeDate->getConfigTimezone());
  $now = new \DateTime('now', $timezone);
  $day = strtolower($now->format('l'));
  return array_push($identities, $day);
}
```

The getIdentities method has been implemented in a way to ensure caching of this block is considered in a relation to product identity as well as the day of the week.

We then create the <MODULE_DIR>/view/frontend/requirejs-config.js file, as follows:

```
var config = {
  map: {
    '*': {
      cutoffAt: 'Magelicious_Catalog/js/cutoff'
    }
  }
};
```

This registers the cutoffAt component with Magento, which points to our module's cutoff.js file.

We then create the <MODULE_DIR>/view/frontend/web/js/cutoff.js file, as follows:

```
define([
    'jquery',
    'uiComponent',
    'ko',
    'moment'
], function ($, Component, ko, moment) {
    'use strict';
    return Component.extend({
      defaults: {
        template: 'Magelicious_Catalog/cutoff',
        expiresAt: null,
        timerHide: false,
        timerHours: null,
```

```
      timerMinutes: null,
      timerSeconds: null,
    },
    initialize: function () {
      this._super();
      this.countdown(this);
      return this;
    },
    initObservable: function () {
      this._super()
        .observe('timerHide timerHours timerMinutes timerSeconds');
      return this;
    },
    countdown: function (self) { /* ... */ }
  });
}
);
```

Our JS component `template` value points to
`<MODULE_DIR>/view/frontend/web/template/cutoff.html`, which we will soon
address. `expiresAt` is the only real option that is expected to be passed on when the
component is initialized. The observable `timer*` options will be used internally to control
the functionality of our component.

The `countdown` function is further implemented, as follows:

```
countdown: function (self) {
  var today = moment(new Date());
  setInterval(function () {
    self.expiresAt = moment(self.expiresAt).subtract(1, 'seconds');
    var milliseconds = moment(self.expiresAt, 'DD/MM/YYYY
HH:mm:ss').diff(moment(today, 'DD/MM/YYYY HH:mm:ss'));
    var duration = moment.duration(milliseconds);
    self.timerHours(duration.hours() >= 0 ? duration.hours() : 0);
    self.timerMinutes(duration.minutes() >= 0 ? duration.minutes() : 0);
    self.timerSeconds(duration.seconds() >= 0 ? duration.seconds() : 0);
    if (self.timerHours() == 0
      && self.timerMinutes() == 0
      && self.timerSeconds() == 0
    ) {
      self.timerHide(true);
    }
  }, 1000);
}
```

This here is the gist of our *same day delivery* functionality. Using the core JS `setInterval` method, we set up a simple *per-second* counter. With the few lines of code wrapped within `setInterval`, we control our observable `timer*` options bound to our `cutoff.html` template. This, in turn, results in the visual countdown effect.

We then create the `<MODULE_DIR>/view/frontend/web/template/cutoff.html` file, as follows:

```
<span class="cutoff-component" data-bind="ifnot: timerHide">
  <span translate="''You have'"></span>
  <span class="timer">
    <span class="timer-part timer-part-hours">
      <span class="numeric" data-bind="text: timerHours"></span>
      <span class="label" data-bind="i18n: 'hours'"></span>
    </span>
    <span class="timer-part timer-part-minutes">
      <span class="numeric" data-bind="text: timerMinutes"></span>
      <span class="label" data-bind="i18n: 'minutes'"></span>
    </span>
    <span class="timer-part timer-part-seconds">
      <span class="numeric" data-bind="text: timerSeconds"></span>
      <span class="label" data-bind="i18n: 'seconds'"></span>
    </span>
  </span>
  <span translate="''to catch our same day delivery offer.'"></span>
</span>
```

This is the template file behind our JS component. We see all those `timer*` options being bounded to proper `span` elements. Wrapping every `timer*` option in its own `span` allows for potential flexibility around styling later on.

 See `https://devdocs.magento.com/guides/v2.2/ui_comp_guide/concepts/knockout-bindings.html` for a list of Magento custom Knockout.js bindings.

We then create the `<MODULE_DIR>/view/frontend/templates/product/view/cutoff.phtml` file, as follows:

```
<?php /* @var \Magelicious\Catalog\Block\Product\View\Cutoff $block */ ?>
<?php $jsonHelper = $this->helper('Magento\Framework\Json\Helper\Data'); ?>

<div class="cutoff" data-bind="scope:'cutoff-scope'">
  <!-- ko template: getTemplate() --><!-- /ko -->
</div>
```

```
<script type="text/x-magento-init">
  {
    ".cutoff": {
      "Magento_Ui/js/core/app": {
        "components": {
          "cutoff-scope": {
            "component": "cutoffAt",
            "expiresAt": <?= /* @escapeNotVerified */
$jsonHelper->jsonEncode($block->getCutoffAt()) ?>
          }
        }
      }
    }
  }
</script>
```

This is the template file that initializes our JS component. With this file in place, we can finally glue things together by amending the body element of the `<MODULE_DIR>/view/frontend/layout/catalog_product_view.xml` file, as follows:

```
<referenceBlock name="product.info.extrahint">
  <block name="cutoff"
      class="Magelicious\Catalog\Block\Product\View\Cutoff"
      template="Magelicious_Catalog::product/view/cutoff.phtml">
  </block>
</referenceBlock>
```

The final *product view* page result should look like this:

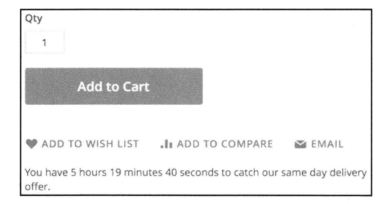

Once the timer reaches **0 hours 0 minutes 0 seconds**, it should disappear.

Flagging new products

We have been asked to add a functionality that flags every new product shown on the storefront *category view* and *product view* pages with a **[NEW]** prefix in front of its name. *New* implies anything within the *5 days* of the product's `created_at` value.

Luckily for us, we can easily control a product's name via an `after` plugin on a product's `getName` method. All it takes is to define an `afterGetName` plugin with a *category view and product view pages* constraint, further filtered by a `created_at` constraint.

To register the plugin, we start by creating the `<MODULE_DIR>/etc/frontend/di.xml` file with content, as follows:

```
<config>
  <type name="Magento\Catalog\Api\Data\ProductInterface">
    <plugin name="newProductFlag"
type="Magelicious\Catalog\Plugin\NewProductFlag"/>
  </type>
</config>
```

We then create the `<MODULE_DIR>/Plugin/NewProductFlag.php` file with content, as follows:

```
namespace Magelicious\Catalog\Plugin;

class NewProductFlag
{
  protected $request;
  protected $localeDate;

  public function __construct(
    \Magento\Framework\App\RequestInterface $request,
    \Magento\Framework\Stdlib\DateTime\TimezoneInterface $localeDate
  )
  {
    $this->request = $request;
    $this->localeDate = $localeDate;
  }

  public function afterGetName(\Magento\Catalog\Api\Data\ProductInterface
$subject, $result)
  {
    $pages = ['catalog_product_view', 'catalog_category_view'];

    if (in_array($this->request->getFullActionName(), $pages)) {
      $timezone = new
```

```
\DateTimeZone($this->localeDate->getConfigTimezone());
        $now = new \DateTime('now', $timezone);
        $createdAt = \DateTime::createFromFormat('Y-m-d H:i:s',
$subject->getCreatedAt(), $timezone);
        if ($now->diff($createdAt)->days < 5) {
          return __('[NEW] ') . $result;
        }
    }

    return $result;
  }
}
```

The `afterGetName` is our `after` plugin targeting the product's `getName` method. Using the `request`'s `getFullActionName` method, we make sure our plugin is constrained to only `catalog_product_view` and `catalog_category_view` pages, or else the original product name is returned. The use of the proper timezone and `diff` method assures that we further filter down to only those products that we consider *new*. Clearing the cache at this point should allow our functionality to kick in.

The final result should look like this:

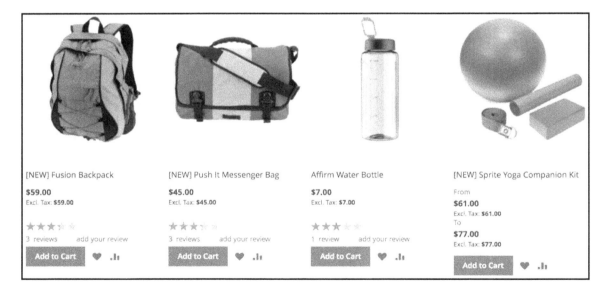

Summary

In this chapter, we have built three distinctive functionalities, all of which relate to the catalog part of Magento. Though very lightweight, they stand to show how easily Magento can be extended with new features without really overriding any of the core files. Using plugins and JS components are merely some of the approaches we might take. Quite often, we will find that a single requirement might be delivered with more than one approach. The main guiding rule for our code should always be: *use the least intrusive.* Catalog functionality plays a major role in the customer conversion process, so our priority should always be *failsafe when possible.*

Moving forward, we are going to take a look at some of the things we can do to customize the checkout.

8
Customizing Checkout Experiences

While the default Magento checkout provides everything a shop needs to complete a transaction successfully, there are details specific to the individual businesses that often need to be addressed. A great deal of these details often relate to checkout customizations that allow for the capturing of additional information or engaging customers in agreements and subscription activities.

Moving forward, we are going to take a look at the following:

- Passing data to the checkout
- Adding order notes to the checkout

Technical requirements

You will need to have basic knowledge of PHP, OOP, JavaScript, and XML. You will also need Apache, MySQL, and AMPPS installed on your system to execute the codes.

The code files of this chapter can be found on GitHub:
`https://github.com/PacktPublishing/Magento-2-Quick-Start-Guide`.

Check out the following video to see the Code in Action:

`http://bit.ly/2PHMwqX`.

Passing data to the checkout

Unlike the mostly static CMS, category, and product pages, the checkout page has a more dynamic nature. It is an application on its own, primarily constructed out of JS components, which further utilize Magento's API endpoints to move us through the checkout steps. Magento's `Magento\Checkout\Model\CompositeConfigProvider` type allows us to push the necessary server-side information easily to the `uiComponent` of the storefronts.

A quick lookup for the `name="configProviders"` string across the content of `di.xml` in the `<MAGENTO_DIR>` directory reveals dozen of definitions. A closer look at the `<MAGENTO_DIR>/module-tax/etc/frontend/di.xml` reveals the following:

```
<type name="Magento\Checkout\Model\CompositeConfigProvider">
  <arguments>
    <argument name="configProviders" xsi:type="array">
      <item name="tax_config_provider"
xsi:type="object">Magento\Tax\Model\TaxConfigProvider</item>
    </argument>
  </arguments>
</type>
```

We are essentially injecting new items under the `configProviders` argument of the `Magento\Checkout\Model\CompositeConfigProvider` type. The implementation of a custom config provider, such as the `Magento\Tax\Model\TaxConfigProvider`, must implement the `Magento\Checkout\Model\ConfigProviderInterface`. The underlying `getConfig` method returns an array of key-value mappings, such as:

```
return [
    'isDisplayShippingPriceExclTax' =>
$this->isDisplayShippingPriceExclTax(),
    'isDisplayShippingBothPrices' => $this->isDisplayShippingBothPrices(),
    'reviewShippingDisplayMode' => $this->getDisplayShippingMode(),
    /* ... */
];
```

These, in turn, become available to the `uiComponent`, as observed in `<MAGENTO_DIR>/module-tax/view/frontend/web/js/view/checkout/shipping_method/price.js`:

```
isDisplayShippingPriceExclTax:
window.checkoutConfig.isDisplayShippingPriceExclTax,
isDisplayShippingBothPrices:
window.checkoutConfig.isDisplayShippingBothPrices,
```

We can see the values returned by the `getConfig` method now available under the JavaScript `window.checkoutConfig` object. This is a simple mechanism by which we can push our server-side data to our storefront when a page loads.

> To understand checkout modifications better, we should familiarize ourselves with the content of the `window.checkoutConfig` object.

Adding order notes to the checkout

Now that we understand the mechanism behind the `window.checkoutConfig` object, let's put it to use by creating a small module that adds *order notes* functionality to the checkout. Our work is to be done as part of the `Magelicious_OrderNotes` module, with the final visual outcome, as follows:

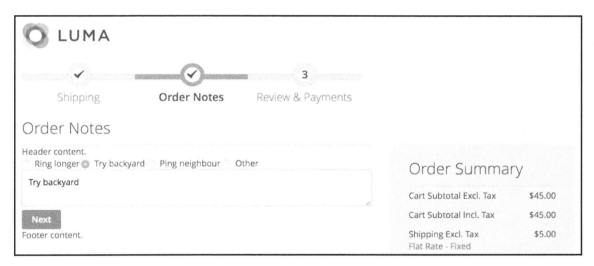

The idea behind the module is to provide a customer with an option of putting a note against their order. On top of that, we also provide a *standard range of possible notes* to choose from.

Assuming we have defined `registration.php`, `composer.json`, and `etc/module.xml` as basic module files, we can deal with the more specific details of our `Magelicious_OrderNotes` module.

We start by defining the `<MODULE_DIR>/Setup/InstallSchema.php` with content, as follows:

```
namespace Magelicious\OrderNotes\Setup;
class InstallSchema implements
\Magento\Framework\Setup\InstallSchemaInterface
{
  public function install(
    \Magento\Framework\Setup\SchemaSetupInterface $setup,
    \Magento\Framework\Setup\ModuleContextInterface $context
  ) {
    $connection = $setup->getConnection();

    $connection->addColumn(
      $setup->getTable('quote'),
      'order_notes',
      [
        'type' => \Magento\Framework\DB\Ddl\Table::TYPE_TEXT,
        'nullable' => true,
        'comment' => 'Order Notes'
      ]
    );

    $connection->addColumn(
      $setup->getTable('sales_order'),
      'order_notes',
      [
        'type' => \Magento\Framework\DB\Ddl\Table::TYPE_TEXT,
        'nullable' => true,
        'comment' => 'Order Notes'
      ]
    );
  }
}
```

Our `InstallSchema` script creates the necessary `order_notes` column in both the `quote` and `sales_order` tables. This is where we will store the value of the customer's checkout note, if there is any.

We then define the `<MODULE_DIR>/etc/frontend/routes.xml` with content, as follows:

```
<config>
  <router id="standard">
```

```
    <route id="ordernotes" frontName="ordernotes">
      <module name="Magelicious_OrderNotes"/>
    </route>
  </router>
</config>
```

The `route` definition here ensures that Magento will recognize HTTP requests starting with `ordernotes`, and look for controller actions within our module.

We then define the `<MODULE_DIR>/Controller/Index.php` with content, as follows:

```
namespace Magelicious\OrderNotes\Controller;

abstract class Index extends \Magento\Framework\App\Action\Action
{
}
```

This is merely an *empty* base class, for our soon-to-follow controller action.

We then define the `<MODULE_DIR>/Controller/Index/Process.php` with content, as follows:

```
namespace Magelicious\OrderNotes\Controller\Index;

class Process extends \Magelicious\OrderNotes\Controller\Index
{
  protected $checkoutSession;
  protected $logger;

  public function __construct(
    \Magento\Framework\App\Action\Context $context,
    \Magento\Checkout\Model\Session $checkoutSession,
    \Psr\Log\LoggerInterface $logger
  )
  {
    $this->checkoutSession = $checkoutSession;
    $this->logger = $logger;
    parent::__construct($context);
  }

  public function execute()
  {
    // implement...
  }
}
```

This controller action should catch any HTTP `ordernotes/index/process` requests. We then extend the `execute` method, as follows:

```
public function execute()
{
  $result = [];
  try {
    if ($notes = $this->getRequest()->getParam('order_notes', null)) {
      $quote = $this->checkoutSession->getQuote();
      $quote->setOrderNotes($notes);
      $quote->save();
      $result[$quote->getId()];
    }
  } catch (\Exception $e) {
    $this->logger->critical($e);
    $result = [
      'error' => __('Something went wrong.'),
      'errorcode' => $e->getCode(),
    ];
  }
  $resultJson =
$this->resultFactory->create(\Magento\Framework\Controller\ResultFactory::T
YPE_JSON);
  $resultJson->setData($result);
  return $resultJson;
}
```

This is where we are storing the order notes on our quote object. Later on, we will pull this onto our sales order object. We further define the `<MODULE_DIR>/etc/frontend/di.xml` with content, as follows:

```
<config>
  <type name="Magento\Checkout\Model\CompositeConfigProvider">
    <arguments>
      <argument name="configProviders" xsi:type="array">
        <item name="order_notes_config_provider" xsi:type="object">
          Magelicious\OrderNotes\Model\ConfigProvider
        </item>
      </argument>
    </arguments>
  </type>
</config>
```

We are registering our configuration provider here. The `order_notes_config_provider` must be unique. We then define the `<MODULE_DIR>/Model/ConfigProvider.php` with content, as follows:

```php
namespace Magelicious\OrderNotes\Model;
class ConfigProvider implements
\Magento\Checkout\Model\ConfigProviderInterface
{
  public function getConfig()
  {
    return [
      'orderNotes' => [
        'title' => __('Order Notes'),
        'header' => __('Header content.'),
        'footer' => __('Footer content.'),
        'options' => [
          ['code' => 'ring', 'value' => __('Ring longer')],
          ['code' => 'backyard', 'value' => __('Try backyard')],
          ['code' => 'neighbour', 'value' => __('Ping neighbour')],
          ['code' => 'other', 'value' => __('Other')],
        ]
      ]
    ];
  }
}
```

This is the implementation of our `order_notes_config_provider` configuration provider. We can pretty much return any array structure we wish. The top-level `orderNotes` will be accessible later via JS components as `window.checkoutConfig.orderNotes`. We further define the `<MODULE_DIR>/view/frontend/layout/checkout_index_index.xml` with content, as follows:

```xml
<page>
  <body>
    <referenceBlock name="checkout.root">
      <arguments>
        <argument name="jsLayout" xsi:type="array">
          <item name="components" xsi:type="array">
            <item name="checkout" xsi:type="array">
              <item name="children" xsi:type="array">
                <item name="steps" xsi:type="array">
                  <item name="children" xsi:type="array">
                    <item name="order-notes" xsi:type="array">
                      <item name="component" xsi:type="string">
                        Magelicious_OrderNotes/js/view/order-notes
                      </item>
```

```
            <item name="sortOrder" xsi:type="string">2</item>
            <!-- closing tags -->
```

There is quite a nesting structure here. Our order notes component is being injected under the `children` component of the checkout's `steps` component.

We then define the `<MODULE_DIR>/view/frontend/web/js/view/order-notes.js` with content, as follows:

```
define([
  'ko',
  'uiComponent',
  'underscore',
  'Magento_Checkout/js/model/step-navigator',
  'jquery',
  'mage/translate',
  'mage/url'
], function (ko, Component, _, stepNavigator, $, $t, url) {
  'use strict';
  let checkoutConfigOrderNotes = window.checkoutConfig.orderNotes;
  return Component.extend({
    defaults: {
      template: 'Magelicious_OrderNotes/order/notes'
    },
    isVisible: ko.observable(true),
    initialize: function () {
      // TODO
    },
    navigate: function () {
      // TODO
    },
    navigateToNextStep: function () {
      // TODO
    }
  });
});
```

This is our `uiComponent`, powered by Knockout. The `template` configuration points to the physical location of the `.html` file that is used as a component's template. The `navigate` and `navigateToNextStep` are responsible for navigation between the checkout steps during checkout. Let's extend the `initialize` function further, as follows:

```
initialize: function () {
  this._super();
  stepNavigator.registerStep(
    'order_notes',
    null,
```

```
      $t('Order Notes'),
      this.isVisible,
      _.bind(this.navigate, this),
      15
    );
    return this;
  }
```

We use the `initialize` method to register our `order_notes` step with the
`stepNavigator`.

Let's extend the `navigateToNextStep` function further, as follows:

```
navigateToNextStep: function () {
  if ($(arguments[0]).is('form')) {
    $.ajax({
      type: 'POST',
      url: url.build('ordernotes/index/process'),
      data: $(arguments[0]).serialize(),
      showLoader: true,
      complete: function (response) {
        stepNavigator.next();
      }
    });
  }
}
```

We use the `navigateToNextStep` method to persist our data. The AJAX `POST`
`ordernotes/index/process` action should grab the entire form and pass its data along.

Finally, let's add the helper methods for our `.html` template, as follows:

```
getTitle: function () {
  return checkoutConfigOrderNotes.title;
},
getHeader: function () {
  return checkoutConfigOrderNotes.header;
},
getFooter: function () {
  return checkoutConfigOrderNotes.footer;
},
getNotesOptions: function () {
  return checkoutConfigOrderNotes.options;
},
getCheckoutConfigOrderNotesTime: function () {
  return checkoutConfigOrderNotes.time;
},
setOrderNotes: function (valObj, event) {
```

```
    if (valObj.code == 'other') {
      $('[name="order_notes"]').val('');
    } else {
      $('[name="order_notes"]').val(valObj.value);
    }
    return true;
  },
```

These are just some of the helper methods we will bind to within our `.html` template. They merely pull the data out from the `window.checkoutConfig.orderNotes` object.

We then define the `<MODULE_DIR>/view/frontend/web/template/order/notes.html` with content, as follows:

```html
<li id="order_notes" data-bind="fadeVisible: isVisible">
    <div data-bind="text: getTitle()" data-role="title"></div>
    <div id="step-content" data-role="content">
        <div data-bind="text: getHeader()" data-role="header"></div>
        <!-- form -->
        <div data-bind="text: getFooter()" data-role="footer"></div>
    </div>
</li>
```

This is our component template, which gives it a visual structure. We expand it further by replacing the `<!-- form -->` with the following:

```html
<form data-bind="submit: navigateToNextStep" novalidate="novalidate">
  <div data-bind="foreach: getNotesOptions()" class="field choice">
    <input type="radio" name="order[notes]" class="radio"
        data-bind="value: code, click: $parent.setOrderNotes"/>
    <label data-bind="attr: {'for': code}" class="label">
      <span data-bind="text: value"></span>
    </label>
  </div>
  <textarea name="order_notes"></textarea>
  <div class="actions-toolbar">
    <div class="primary">
      <button data-role="opc-continue" type="submit" class="button action
continue primary">
        <span><!-- ko i18n: 'Next'--><!-- /ko --></span>
      </button>
    </div>
  </div>
</form>
```

The form itself is relatively simple, though it requires some knowledge of Knockout. Understanding the data binding is quite important. It allows us to bind not just text and the HTML values of HTML elements, but other attributes as well, such as the `click`.

We then define the `<MODULE_DIR>/etc/webapi_rest/events.xml` with content, as follows:

```
<config>
  <event name="sales_model_service_quote_submit_before">
    <observer name="orderNotesToOrder"
      instance="Magelicious\OrderNotes\Observer\SaveOrderNotesToOrder"
      shared="false"/>
  </event>
</config>
```

The `sales_model_service_quote_submit_before` event is chosen because it allows us to gain access to both *quote* and *order* objects easily at the right time in the order creation process.

We then define the `<MODULE_DIR>/Observer/SaveOrderNotesToOrder.php` with content, as follows:

```
namespace Magelicious\OrderNotes\Observer;

class SaveOrderNotesToOrder implements
\Magento\Framework\Event\ObserverInterface
{
  public function execute(\Magento\Framework\Event\Observer $observer)
  {
    $event = $observer->getEvent();
    if ($notes = $event->getQuote()->getOrderNotes()) {
      $event->getOrder()
        ->setOrderNotes($notes)
        ->addStatusHistoryComment('Customer note: ' . $notes);
    }
    return $this;
  }
}
```

Here, we are grabbing the instance of an order object and setting the order notes to the value fetched from the order notes value of a previously stored quote. This makes the customer note appear under the **Comments History** tab of the Magento admin order **View** screen, as follows:

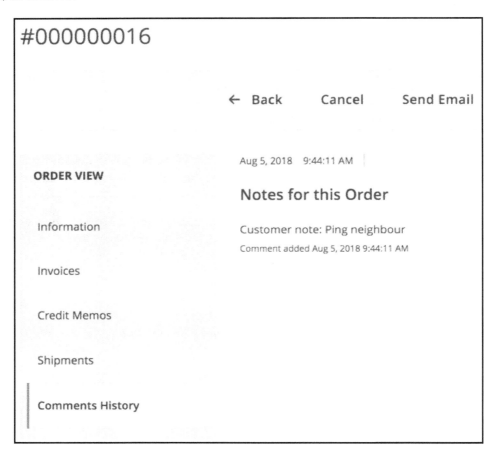

With this, we have finalized our little module. Even though the module's functionality is quite simple, the steps for getting it up and running were somewhat involved.

Summary

In this chapter, we have built a small, but functional, *order notes* module. This allowed us to familiarize ourselves with an important aspect of customizing the checkout experience. The gist of this lies in understanding the `checkout_index_index` layout handle, the JavaScript `window.checkoutConfig` object, and the `uiComponent`.

Failure to deliver consistent and stable checkout experiences is bound to result in a loss of conversions. Given the number and complexity of the components involved, it is best to keep the number of checkout customizations to a minimum.

Moving forward, we are going to take a look at some of the things we can do regarding the customization of customer interactions.

9
Customizing Customer Interactions

Along with the catalog and checkout, customer-related functionality is central to Magento. The customer's **My Account** area allows control over addresses, orders, billing agreements, product wishlists, product reviews, newsletter subscriptions, and more. Customizing customer functionality often includes changes to the **Sign In** and **Create an Account** processes, as well as modifying existing, or adding new functionality under the **My Account** area.

Depending on the dynamics and intricacy of our functionality, JS components are often friendlier solutions than server-side PHTML templates. They allow us to engage the customer without necessarily reloading entire pages, thus improving the overall customer experience. As with any client to server-side communication, the question of passing and updating the data remains to be addressed. This is where we turn our focus to Magento's *section* mechanism.

Moving forward we are going to take a look at the following:

- Understanding the section mechanism
- Adding contact preferences to customer accounts
- Adding contact preferences to the checkout

Technical requirements

You will need to have basic knowledge of PHP, OOP, JavaScript, and XML. You will also need Apache, MySQL, and AMPPS installed on your system to execute the codes.

The code files of this chapter can be found on GitHub:
`https://github.com/PacktPublishing/Magento-2-Quick-Start-Guide`.

Check out the following video to see the Code in Action:

`http://bit.ly/2NQFB1f`.

Understanding the section mechanism

Our previous chapter touched upon *config providers* and the `window.checkoutConfig` object; a mechanism by which we can push our server-side data to our storefront when a page loads. The `section` mechanism allows us to push data to a browser page upon *any named* HTTP POST request.

Let's take a quick look at the `<MAGENTO_DIR>/module-review/etc/frontend/sections.xml` file:

```
<action name="review/product/post">
  <section name="review"/>
</action>
```

The definition provided here is to be interpreted as: "any storefront HTTP POST `review/product/post` request is to trigger a `review` section load," where `review` *section load* means Magento triggering an additional AJAX request following the completion of an observed HTTP POST. The result of this *section load* action, in this case, is the refresh of section data, retrievable via `customerData.get('review')`, as we will soon see.

Now let's take a look at the `<MAGENTO_DIR>/module-review/etc/frontend/di.xml` file:

```xml
<type name="Magento\Customer\CustomerData\SectionPoolInterface">
  <arguments>
    <argument name="sectionSourceMap" xsi:type="array">
      <item name="review"
xsi:type="string">Magento\Review\CustomerData\Review</item>
    </argument>
  </arguments>
</type>
```

We are essentially injecting new items under the `sectionSourceMap` argument of the `Magento\Customer\CustomerData\SectionPoolInterface` type. The implementation of a custom section, such as the `Magento\Review\CustomerData\Review`, must implement the `Magento\Customer\CustomerData\SectionSourceInterface`. The underlying `getSectionData` method returns an array of key-value mappings, such as:

```php
return [
    'nickname' => '',
    'title' => '',
    'detail' => ''
]
```

These, in turn, become available to the `uiComponent`, as observed in the partial `<MAGENTO_DIR>/module-review/view/frontend/web/js/view/review.js` file:

```js
define([
  'uiComponent',
  'Magento_Customer/js/customer-data',
  'Magento_Customer/js/view/customer'
], function (Component, customerData) {
  'use strict';

  return Component.extend({
    initialize: function () {
      this.review = customerData.get('review') ...
    },

    nickname: function () {
      return this.review().nickname ...
    }
  });
});
```

The get method of the customerData object can be used to fetch the sectionSourceMap data, such as customerData.get('review'). This data is refreshed every time an HTTP POST is made to the review/product/post route. This is because following any HTTP POST review/product/post, Magento will trigger an HTTP GET customer/section/load/?sections=review&update_section_id=true&_=1533836 467415, which in turn updates customerData accordingly.

Adding contact preferences to customer accounts

Now that we understand the mechanism behind the customerData object and the section load, let's put it to use by creating a small module that adds *contact preferences* functionality under the customer's **My Account** area, as well as under the checkout. Our work is to be done as part of the Magelicious_ContactPreferences module, with the final visual outcome as follows:

By contrast, the customer's checkout area would show contact preferences, as follows:

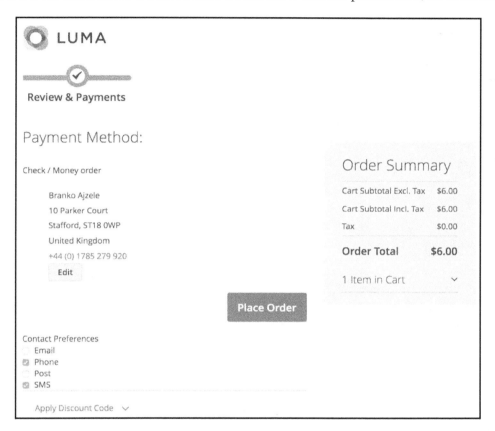

The idea behind the module is to provide a customer with an option of choosing preferred contact preferences, so that a merchant may follow up with the delivery process accordingly.

Assuming we have defined registration.php, composer.json, and etc/module.xml as basic module files, we can deal with the more specific details of our Magelicious_ContactPreferences module.

We start by defining the <MODULE_DIR>/Setup/InstallData.php, as follows:

```
$customerSetup = $this->customerSetupFactory->create(['setup' => $setup]);

$customerSetup->addAttribute(
  \Magento\Customer\Model\Customer::ENTITY,
  'contact_preferences',
```

```
    [
        'type' => 'varchar',
        'label' => 'Contact Preferences',
        'input' => 'multiselect',
        'source' =>
\Magelicious\ContactPreferences\Model\Entity\Attribute\Source\Contact\Prefe
rences::class,
        'required' => 0,
        'sort_order' => 99,
        'position' => 99,
        'system' => 0,
        'visible' => 1,
        'global' =>
\Magento\Catalog\Model\ResourceModel\Eav\Attribute::SCOPE_GLOBAL,
    ]
);

$contactPreferencesAttr = $customerSetup
    ->getEavConfig()
    ->getAttribute(
        \Magento\Customer\Model\Customer::ENTITY,
        'contact_preferences'
    );

$contactPreferencesAttr->setData('used_in_forms', ['adminhtml_customer']);
$contactPreferencesAttr->save();
```

We are instructing Magento to create a `multiselect` type of attribute. The attribute becomes visible under the Magento admin area, with a customer editing screen as follows:

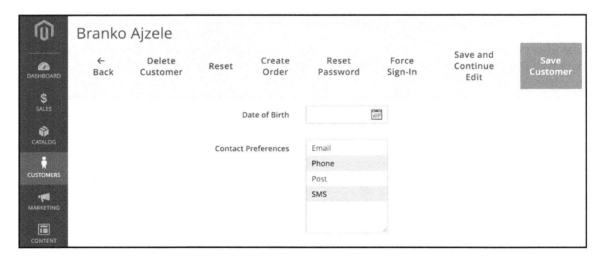

We then define
the `<MODULE_DIR>/Model/Entity/Attribute/Source/Contact/Preferences.php`,
as follows:

```
namespace
Magelicious\ContactPreferences\Model\Entity\Attribute\Source\Contact;

class Preferences extends
\Magento\Eav\Model\Entity\Attribute\Source\AbstractSource
{
  const VALUE_EMAIL = 'email';
  const VALUE_PHONE = 'phone';
  const VALUE_POST = 'post';
  const VALUE_SMS = 'sms';

  public function getAllOptions()
  {
    return [
      ['label' => __('Email'), 'value' => self::VALUE_EMAIL],
      ['label' => __('Phone'), 'value' => self::VALUE_PHONE],
      ['label' => __('Post'), 'value' => self::VALUE_POST],
      ['label' => __('SMS'), 'value' => self::VALUE_SMS],
    ];
  }
}
```

These are the contact preference options we want to provide as our attribute source. We will use this class not just for installation, but later on as well.

We then define the `<MODULE_DIR>/etc/frontend/routes.xml`, as follows:

```
<config>
  <router id="standard">
    <route id="customer" frontName="customer">
      <module name="Magelicious_ContactPreferences"
before="Magento_Customer"/>
    </route>
  </router>
</config>
```

Unlike our route definitions in previous chapters, here we are using an already existing route name `customer`. The attribute before it allows us to *insert* our module before the `Magento_Customer` module, allowing us to respond to the same `customer/*` routes. We should be very careful with this approach, not to *detach* some of the existing controller actions. In our case, we are only doing this so that we might use the `customer/contact/preferences` URL later on.

We then define the `<MODULE_DIR>/Controller/Contact/Preferences.php`, as follows:

```php
namespace Magelicious\ContactPreferences\Controller\Contact;

class Preferences extends \Magento\Customer\Controller\AbstractAccount
{
  public function execute()
  {
    if ($this->getRequest()->isPost()) {
      $resultJson =
$this->resultFactory->create(\Magento\Framework\Controller\ResultFactory::TYPE_JSON);
      if ($this->getRequest()->getParam('load')) {
        // Merely for triggering "contact_preferences" section
      } else {
        // SAVE PREFERENCES
      }
      return $resultJson;
    } else {
      $resultPage =
$this->resultFactory->create(\Magento\Framework\Controller\ResultFactory::TYPE_PAGE);
      $resultPage->getConfig()->getTitle()->set(__('My Contact
Preferences'));
      return $resultPage;
    }
  }
}
```

This is the only controller action we will have. We will use the same action for handling three different intents. This is not an ideal example of how one should write code in this scenario, but it is a compact one. The first intent we will handle is the *section load trigger*, the second is the actual *preference save*, and the third is the *page load*. These will become clear as we move forward.

We then replace the SAVE PREFERENCES comment with the following:

```php
// \Magento\Framework\App\Action\Context $context
// \Magento\Customer\Model\Session $customerSession
// \Magento\Customer\Api\CustomerRepositoryInterface $customerRepository
// \Psr\Log\LoggerInterface $logger

try {
  $preferences = implode(',',
    array_keys(
      array_filter($this->getRequest()->getParams(), function ($_checked,
```

```
$_preference) {
        return filter_var($_checked, FILTER_VALIDATE_BOOLEAN);
    }, ARRAY_FILTER_USE_BOTH)
  )
);
$customer =
$this->customerRepository->getById($this->customerSession->getCustomerId())
;
  $customer->setCustomAttribute('contact_preferences', $preferences);
  $this->customerRepository->save($customer);
  $this->messageManager->addSuccessMessage(__('Successfully saved contact
preferences.'));
} catch (\Exception $e) {
  $this->logger->critical($e);
  $this->messageManager->addErrorMessage(__('Error saving contact
preferences.'));
}
```

Here we are handling the actual saving of the chosen contact preferences. The request parameters are expected to be in the `<preference_name>=<true|false>` format. We use the `implode` to turn the incoming request and pass it onto the repository's `setCustomAttribute` method. This is because, by default, Magento stores the multiselect attribute as a comma-separated string in the database. The `addSuccessMessage` and `addErrorMessage` calls are interesting here. One might expect that we would return these messages as part of a JSON response. But, we don't really need a JSON response body here. This is because Magento has the `messages` section defined under `<MAGENTO_DIR>/module-theme/etc/frontend/sections.xml` as `<action name="*">`. What this means is that messages get refreshed upon every section load and, since our controller action is mapped in our own `sections.xml`, the load of our section will also load messages.

We then define the `<MODULE_DIR>/view/frontend/layout/customer_account.xml`, as follows:

```
<page>
  <body>
    <referenceBlock name="customer_account_navigation">
      <block class="Magento\Customer\Block\Account\SortLinkInterface"
name="customer-account-navigation-contact-preferences-link">
        <arguments>
          <argument name="path"
xsi:type="string">customer/contact/preferences</argument>
          <argument name="label" xsi:type="string" translate="true">My
Contact Preferences</argument>
          <argument name="sortOrder" xsi:type="number">230</argument>
        </arguments>
```

```
      </block>
     </referenceBlock>
   </body>
</page>
```

The definitions here inject a new menu item under the customer's **My Account** screen. The `customer_account_navigation` block, originally defined under `<MAGENTO_DIR>/module-customer/view/frontend/layout/customer_account.xml`, is in charge of rendering the sidebar menu. By injecting the new block of `Magento\Customer\Block\Account\SortLinkInterface` type, we can easily add new menu items.

We then define the `<MODULE_DIR>/view/frontend/layout/customer_contact_preferences.xml`, as follows:

```
<page>
  <update handle="customer_account"/>
  <body>
    <referenceContainer name="content">
      <block name="contact_preferences"
template="Magelicious_ContactPreferences::customer/contact/preferences.phtm
l" cacheable="false"/>
    </referenceContainer>
  </body>
</page>
```

This is the block that will get loaded into the content area of a page, once we click on our newly added **My Contact Preferences** link. Since the only role of the `contact_preferences` block will be to load the JS component, we omit the class definition that we would normally have on custom blocks.

We then define the `<MODULE_DIR>/view/frontend/templates/customer/contact/preferences.phtml`, as follows:

```
<div class="contact-preferences" data-bind="scope:'contact-preferences-
scope'">
  <!-- ko template: getTemplate() --><!-- /ko -->
</div>

<script type="text/x-magento-init">
  {
    ".contact-preferences": {
      "Magento_Ui/js/core/app": {
```

```
        "components": {
          "contact-preferences-scope": {
            "component": "contactPreferences"
          }
        }
      }
    }
  }
}
</script>
```

The only purpose of the template here is to load the JS `contactPreferences` component. We can see that no data is passed from the server-side `.phtml` template to the JS component. We will use the `section` and `customerData` mechanisms later on for that.

We then define the `<MODULE_DIR>/view/frontend/requirejs-config.js`, as follows:

```
var config = {
  map: {
    '*': {
      contactPreferences: 'Magelicious_ContactPreferences/js/view/contact-
preferences'
    }
  }
};
```

Here we map the component name, `contactPreferences`, to its physical location in our module directory.

We then define the `<MODULE_DIR>/view/frontend/web/js/view/contact-preferences.js`, as follows:

```
define([
  'uiComponent',
  'jquery',
  'mage/url',
  'Magento_Customer/js/customer-data'
], function (Component, $, url, customerData) {
  'use strict';
  let contactPreferences = customerData.get('contact_preferences');
  return Component.extend({
    defaults: {
      template: 'Magelicious_ContactPreferences/contact-preferences'
    },
    initialize: function () { /* ... */ },

    isCustomerLoggedIn: function () {
      return contactPreferences().isCustomerLoggedIn;
```

```
    },
    getSelectOptions: function () {
      return contactPreferences().selectOptions;
    },
    saveContactPreferences: function () { /* ... */ }
  });
});
```

This is our JS component, the core of our client-side functionality. We inject the `Magento_Customer/js/customer-data` component as a `customerData` object. This gives us access to data we are pushing from the server side via the `getSectionData` method of the `Magelicious\ContactPreferences\CustomerData\Preferences` class. The string value `contact_preferences` passed to the `get` method of the `customerData` object must match the item `name` under the `sectionSourceMap` of our `di.xml` definition.

Let's extend the `initialize` function further, as follows:

```
initialize: function () {
  this._super();
  $.ajax({
    type: 'POST',
    url: url.build('customer/contact/preferences'),
    data: {'load': true},
    showLoader: true
  });
}
```

The addition of an AJAX request call within the component's `initialize` method is more of a trick to trigger the `contact_preferences` section load in our case. We are doing it simply because sections do not load on HTTP GET requests, as that might load the same `customer/contact/preferences` page. Rather, they load on HTTP POST events. This way we ensure that the `contact_preferences` section will load when our component is initialized, thus providing it with the necessary data. We are far from saying that this is a recommended approach for general JS component development, though.

Let's extend the `saveContactPreferences` function further, as follows:

```
saveContactPreferences: function () {
  let preferences = {};

  $('.contact_preference').children(':checkbox').each(function () {
    preferences[$(this).attr('name')] = $(this).attr('checked') ? true :
false;
  });

  $.ajax({
```

```
      type: 'POST',
      url: url.build('customer/contact/preferences'),
      data: preferences,
      showLoader: true,
      complete: function (response) {
        // some actions...
      }
    });

    return true;
  }
```

The `saveContactPreferences` method will be triggered every time a customer clicks on the contact preference on the storefront, whether it is an act of checking or unchecking individual contact preferences.

We then define the `<MODULE_DIR>/view/frontend/web/template/contact-preferences.html`, as follows:

```
<div data-bind="if: isCustomerLoggedIn()">
  <div data-role="title" data-bind="i18n: 'Contact Preferences'"></div>
  <div data-role="content">
    <div class="contact_preference" repeat="foreach: getSelectOptions(),
item: '$option'">
      <input type="checkbox"
             click="saveContactPreferences"
             ko-checked="$option().checked"
             attr="name: $option().value"/>
      <label text="$option().label" attr="for: $option().value"/>
    </div>
  </div>
</div>
```

The HTML defined here visually sets our component. A basic knowledge of Knockout JS is required in order to utilize the `repeat` directive, fed with the array of data coming from the `getSelectOptions` method, which by now we know originates from the server side.

We then define the <MODULE_DIR>/etc/frontend/sections.xml, as follows:

```
<config>
  <action name="customer/contact/preferences">
    <section name="contact_preferences"/>
  </action>
</config>
```

With this, we make the necessary mapping between HTTP
POST customer/contact/preferences requests and the contact_preferences
section we expect to load.

We then define the <MODULE_DIR>/etc/frontend/di.xml, as follows:

```
<config>
  <type name="Magento\Customer\CustomerData\SectionPoolInterface">
    <arguments>
      <argument name="sectionSourceMap" xsi:type="array">
        <item name="contact_preferences"
xsi:type="string">Magelicious\ContactPreferences\CustomerData\Preferences</
item>
      </argument>
    </arguments>
  </type>
</config>
```

Here we inject our contact_preferences section, instructing Magento where to *read its
data from*. With this in place, any HTTP POST customer/contact/preferences request
is expected to trigger a follow-up AJAX POST
customer/section/load/?sections=contact_preferences%2Cmessages&update_s
ection_id=true&_=1533887023603 request that, in turn, returns data much like the
following:

```
{
  "contact_preferences": {
  "selectOptions": [
    {
    "label": "Email",
    "value": "email",
    "checked": true
    },
    { ... }
  ],
  "isCustomerLoggedIn": true,
  "data_id": 1533875246
  },
  "messages": {
```

```
    "messages": [
      {
      "type": "success",
      "text": "Successfully saved contact preferences."
      }
    ],
    "data_id": 1533875246
    }
  }
```

If we were to enable our module at this point, we should be able to see it working under the customer's **My Account** screen. Though simple, the steps of getting everything linked were somewhat involved. The benefit of this approach, where data is sent via the `sections` mechanism, is that our component plays nicely with full-page caching. The needed customer-related data is simply fetched by additional AJAX calls, instead of caching it on a per-customer basis, and thus this bypasses the purpose of full-page caching.

Adding contact preferences to the checkout

With our component now working on the customer's **My Account** page, let's go ahead and add it to the checkout's **Review & Payments** step as well.

By tapping into the `checkout_index_index` layout handle, and nesting our component under the desired `children` element, we can easily add it to the checkout page. We do so with the `<MODULE_DIR>/view/frontend/layout/checkout_index_index.xml` file, as follows:

```
<page>
 <body>
  <referenceBlock name="checkout.root">
   <arguments>
    <argument name="jsLayout" xsi:type="array">
     <item name="components" xsi:type="array">
      <item name="checkout" xsi:type="array">
       <item name="children" xsi:type="array">
        <item name="steps" xsi:type="array">
         <item name="children" xsi:type="array">
          <item name="billing-step" xsi:type="array">
           <item name="children" xsi:type="array">
            <item name="payment" xsi:type="array">
             <item name="children" xsi:type="array">
              <item name="afterMethods" xsi:type="array">
               <item name="children" xsi:type="array">
                <item name="contact-preferences" xsi:type="array">
```

```
                    <item name="component"
 xsi:type="string">Magelicious_ContactPreferences/js/view/contact-
 preferences</item>
                    <!-- closing tags -->
```

The nesting structure of `checkout_index_index.xml` is quite robust. There are several places where we can actually insert our own component. Most of the time, this might be trial and error. In this case, we opted for the `children` area of `afterMethods`. This should position it under the checkout's **Review & Payments** step, right after the payments method list.

Summary

In this chapter, we have built a small module that allowed us to get a greater insight into Magento's `customerData` and *sections* mechanisms. We managed to build a single component, that got used both on the customer's `My Account` page, as well as on the checkout.

With this, we have reached the end of our book. The topics we have covered should be enough to get us going with Magento development, but the sheer size of the platform and the intricate specifics of its individual modules leave plenty more to explore further on. It goes without saying that our journey has merely begun.

Other Books You May Enjoy

If you enjoyed this book, you may be interested in these other books by Packt:

Magento 2 Beginners Guide
Gabriel Guarino

ISBN: 9781785880766

- Build your first web store in Magento 2
- Migrate your development environment to a live store
- Configure your Magento 2 web store the right way, so that your taxes are handled properly
- Create pages with arbitrary content
- Create and manage customer contacts and accounts
- Protect Magento instance admin from unexpected intrusions
- Set up newsletter and transactional emails so that communication from your website corresponds to the website's look and feel
- Make the store look good in terms of PCI compliance

Magento 2 Developer's Guide
Branko Ajzele

ISBN: 9781785886584

- Set up the development and production environment of Magento 2
- Understand the new major concepts and conventions used in Magento 2
- Build a miniature yet fully-functional module from scratch to manage your e-commerce platform efficiently
- Write models and collections to manage and search your entity data
- Dive into backend development such as creating events, observers, cron jobs, logging, profiling, and messaging features
- Get to the core of frontend development such as blocks, templates, layouts, and the themes of Magento 2
- Use token, session, and Oauth token-based authentication via various flavors of API calls, as well as creating your own APIs
- Get to grips with testing Magento modules and custom Magento themes, which forms an integral part of development

Leave a review - let other readers know what you think

Please share your thoughts on this book with others by leaving a review on the site that you bought it from. If you purchased the book from Amazon, please leave us an honest review on this book's Amazon page. This is vital so that other potential readers can see and use your unbiased opinion to make purchasing decisions, we can understand what our customers think about our products, and our authors can see your feedback on the title that they have worked with Packt to create. It will only take a few minutes of your time, but is valuable to other potential customers, our authors, and Packt. Thank you!

Index

www.ingramcontent.com/pod-product-compliance
Lightning Source LLC
Chambersburg PA
CBHW080525060326
40690CB00022B/5030